(Photo by Janet Macoska)

Pop goes Cleveland!

PETER CHAKERIAN

PUBLISHING INFORMATION
Published by
Cleveland Landmarks Press, Inc.
13610 Shaker Boulevard, Suite 503
Cleveland, Ohio 44120-1592

Clevelandlandmarkspress.com
(216) 658 4144

ISBN: 978-0-936760-27-8
LIBRARY OF CONGRESS NUMBER: 2009935273

Cover Design and Graphics by Brittyn J. DeWerth
Interior Design/Layout by John Yasenosky III

Printed by
Bookmasters
Ashland, Ohio

"Cleveland is a place I can commit to: complex, missing something, yearning for more, informed by a checkered but fulsome past, and vulnerable enough to allow hope to triumph over experience."

— Anne Trubek, Associate Professor,
Rhetoric & Composition, Oberlin College
City Vision: Project Cleveland

"As in Lawrence Ferlinghetti's A Coney Island of the Mind, *or Sergey Gandlevsky's* America of the Mind, *a place is as much inside us as it is outside us. Every daily path slowly burns its neural path into our brains, until each of us, a denizen of Cleveland, inescapably, not only lives in Cleveland, but comes to create a Cleveland, to become a Cleveland,* a cleaved land, *a place we cleave to, a place we are inextricably a part of and apart from, a Cleveland, a Cleveland of the mind."*

— Philip Metres, poet

"I got some records from World War Two/ I'll play 'em just like me grand dad do/ He was a rocker and I am, too/ Oh, Cleveland rocks! Yeah, Cleveland rocks!"

— Ian Hunter, Cleveland Rocks

This book is dedicated to the memory of Ruth Jane Chakerian, who taught me to be brave in the face of adversity, nurtured my love of history, non-fiction, and popular culture, and fostered in me a curiosity and appreciation I'll always have for my hometown.

I love you, Mom.

Table of Contents

Foreword

I first approached Cleveland Landmarks Press with the idea to do a book about Northeast Ohio's influence on popular culture nearly two years ago. I figured that because publishers Greg Deegan and Jim Toman were carrying on a 28-year tradition of producing books about Cleveland's landmarks and key events, one established by Toman and partner Dan Cook in 1980, the project seemed a perfect fit.

In our meeting, their passion and commitment to preserve the history of the region was palpable; apparently my own enthusiasm for the subject matter you're about to read was likewise to them, although they did look at me a bit cross-eyed when I first attempted to explain the subject matter.

The idea was a simple one: the region now referred to as "Cleveland Plus" (proclaimed so by the former Greater Cleveland Marketing Alliance) has produced a wealth of talent, artistry, and creativity across multiple disciplines. Cleveland, Akron, Canton, Youngstown, and all points in between have had a profound impact on global popular culture, and certainly not least our own "national fabric."

Sure, keep an eye on your local television news or daily paper, and you'll get the token "they came from Cleveland," "originally from Canton," and "invented in Akron" human interest stories here and there. But the premise explored in full? I couldn't recall such a thing, and I felt an obligation, and I suppose a civic duty, to institutionalize, enshrine, and celebrate these stories all in one place. After all, some of what has emerged from right here in Northeast Ohio has become outright iconic anchored in the mind and heart, if not always so geographically.

Superman. The Wizard of Oz. Rock and Roll. Bob Hope. The Rat Pack. Life Savers. *Monday Night Football.* The environmental movement. *Butch Cassidy and the Sundance Kid.* Freddy Krueger. Nirvana. *Forrest Gump.* Drew Carey. Nine Inch Nails. LeBron James. Even current U.S. President Barack Obama. (Sound like a stretch? The road paved for the Chicago politician to become president happened partially because of what transpired in Northeast Ohio.) What do all of these popular culture touchstones have in common? Northeast Ohio.

The idea that these Northeast Ohio landmarks that could be seen/ heard/ felt/ experienced from anywhere around the world, as well as offer a psychic anchor of sorts right here in the region, was an exciting premise to pursue. I mean, who from Northeast Ohio didn't feel an overwhelming sense of pride during the Opening Ceremonies of the 2008 Beijing Olympics when the cameras panned to children in the stands of Beijing's National "Bird's Nest" Olympic Stadium wearing LeBron James Cleveland Cavaliers jerseys?

That's how the idea for *Pop Goes Cleveland!* was born. But credit where it's due: the idea for this book probably hatched during a couple of happy-hour discussions with an old college pal several years ago. For a time, he was hot on the idea of founding a "Cleveland Pop Culture Museum." Over a few cold beverages, my friend and I kicked our elementary school-like imaginations into high gear and volleyed ideas back and forth about what this museum might be.

How would such a place look? What would be cool to find in such a place? Not long after those discussions, I had a dream of just such a location.

I imagined a building sitting on the Lake Erie shore. It would be filled with related pop culture artifacts and shaped like a Quonset hut and painted like a giant roll of Peppermint Life Savers, the famous candy developed by Cleveland chocolate manufacturer Clarence A. Crane. The giant candy tube would be a stop on the Lolly the Trolley Tour, situated on the lakefront near Burke Lakefront Airport, just a stone's throw from the Rock and Roll Hall of Fame and Museum and the Great Lakes Science Center.

My mind reeled at the idea of kids getting their photos taken outside this "Pop Hall," in front of a gigantic Superman statue, the model superhero created by Clevelanders Joe Shuster and Jerry Siegel. Hey, Superman may have settled in Metropolis, but he was born here, not on planet Krypton.

Visitors to this "Pop Hall" could check out Drew Carey's horn-rimmed glasses and artifacts from the set of his ABC television sitcom; Halle Berry's dress from the Academy Awards, when she won "Best Actress" for *Monster's Ball*; Trent Reznor's mud-covered, smashed synthesizers from Nine Inch Nails' seminal Woodstock 1994 performance; broadcaster Alan Freed's studio microphones; LeBron James' St. Vincent-St. Mary's championship jerseys; Devo's original "energy cone" helmets and outfits; Bob Hope's golf clubs, and hundreds of other artifacts.

Can you imagine visiting a place like this — equal parts cool, quirky, and quintessentially regional?

The next morning, the list of Northeast Ohio icons started to build: Carey, Berry, Reznor, James, Hope, Freed, Tom Hanks, "Chef Boyardee," Tim Russert, Paul Newman. The list literally went on and on. The thoughts snowballed: my mind reasoned that if Philadelphia can have a twelve-foot bronze sculpture of Sylvester Stallone as the Oscar-winning "Rocky Balboa" character, a *fictional* character symbolizing their city's spirit, why couldn't we have something similar in Cleveland?

By the way, *Rocky* has a Cleveland connection. His trainer, "Mickey Goldmill," was portrayed by actor Burgess Meredith, born in Cleveland. Wonder how Balboa would have fared without him?

And why couldn't these pop culture touchstones be celebrated alongside locally based icons like Ghoulardi, Jane Scott, the Michael Stanley Band, and others — people who have created changes to the pop culture landscape locally and, in some cases, nationally, while remaining fixtures of the area?

The snowball continued to roll.

Northeast Ohio residents often downplay their strengths (hard-working, determined) and often turn up the volume on that self-effacing, Midwestern "aw shucks" Clark Kent mentality. Instead of hanging our collective hats on the positive and successful which has emerged from here, we allow re-tread stories of Cleveland going into default, the Kent State shootings, the Cuyahoga River burning, our sports teams flailing, and industry across Northeast Ohio dying out. We allow those images to define us and burrow into our subconscious. And yes, some of these negative views and psychic baggage are perpetuated by the very popular culture and mainstream media we look to celebrate in this book. But some very positive "lemonade" has come from those "lemons" as well.

For example, the modern environmental movement and the "greening" and environmental protection of America points to our burning Cuyahoga River 40 years ago as a catalyst for change. Sure, Cleveland's river burned – *what's it to ya?* What if it hadn't? Ponder that one for a minute.

Life Savers and the Man of Steel are just two of many pop culture symbols and conduits forged here in Cleveland. Both are now worldwide, billion-dollar industries, and ubiquitous in pop culture influence.

I'd still like to see a Northeast Ohio Pop Culture Museum, or "Pop Hall" as my pal once referred to it. I think it could be an important piece to overcoming our inferiority complex and giving us natives the opportunity to teach the next generation of Clevelanders to think about and work to preserve and appreciate our region and its history.

Not being an urban planner or politician, I feared the idea for such a museum could toil in obscurity, another great idea that never quite got off the ground. But being a longtime Cleveland journalist, cheerleader, pop culture enthusiast, and a provocateur of sorts, I realized there was a soapbox I could stand on to deliver this message. And I decided this idea's time was now.

To wit, hopefully someone will read this book, experience an overwhelming epiphany about Northeast Ohio's successes, and use it as a blueprint for a real Northeast Ohio pop culture museum.

Part reference manual, trivia guide, photo album, and love letter, I'd like to think that *Pop Goes Cleveland! The Impact of Cleveland (and Northeast Ohio) on Pop Culture* celebrates the symbiotic relationship between a region and the culture it has helped to define.

For the rest of you, consider this book a much-needed dose of civic pride about the region, a construction of a "Northeast Ohio of the mind," to paraphrase local poet Philip Metres. The overriding message to everyone with Northeast Ohio roots is that anything is possible, even from right here at home.

Peter Chakerian

"Cleveland Skyline"
(Photo by Janet Macoska)

Introduction

In Mark Halliday's poem "Cleveland," the poet and Ohio University professor of English literature imagines a single mother named "Janey" who has "become increasingly realistic in Cleveland . . . where you have to choose which reality to deal with when."

Never mind that Halliday has since suggested that the city of Philadelphia (again?) inspired such an elegy; it remains a bold statement on the power of the imagination and the role it plays for human beings in the midst of turmoil and decline.

Every day, Northeast Ohio residents are inundated with statistics that the region they consider home is a shell of its former self. Once the fifth-largest city in the United States, a manufacturing mecca, and a catch basin for flocks of immigrant populations, Cleveland now bears the brunt of every "Top Ten" list of fattest, dumbest, least desirable, or most dangerous cities in the country. Cleveland, the region's seat, is often the target of these lists. The burning river, city default, growing foreclosures, sports team failures, and race riots are just the beginning of the litany of events that maintains the region's mostly self-inflicted inferiority complex.

Clevelanders, in particular, have not stopped psychoanalyzing themselves since the Cuyahoga River fire 40 years ago. It's a moment that has transcended mythology to become a self-fulfilling prophecy in the minds of many. The words "mistake by the lake," "cursed," "psychiatrist's dream," "end-of-the-line despair," and "land of broken dreams" sit on the pursed lips of many residents, even if they're never uttered. And critics still use these semantics to make Cleveland and the region the butt of jokes to such great effect that even the name *Cleveland* is a loaded one to the rest of the country.

Make no mistake, Northeast Ohio is in the midst of a crisis. That often belies the fact that most residents of this region are good, hard-working, decent, generous, dedicated, creative, and personable Midwesterners with big goals and dreams. But that phenomenon of negative reinforcement about the region doesn't just impact the people who live and work here, it affects people outside the region, carrying forward a negative perception about a place that has offered so much. It speaks to just how powerful the images and messages of popular culture are.

But why not focus on the great things that have come from here as well? The dogged and determined people and ideas which were so big in some cases that they needed to be fully realized in greener pastures? It can be easy to forget that more good than bad has come from this region and that it's a lot cooler and more interesting than its reputation. Northeast Ohio has a rich history of "firsts," inventions, innovations, and a wealth of talent, amazing levels of creativity and intelligence. It can compete with any region in the country.

We can all agree that some of Northeast Ohio's reality has been truly hard to understand and, as Halliday says, "deal with." Here's hoping that this book makes a case for the reality of fantasy and imagination being tantamount to reality itself.

What is Pop Culture?

This is a question that most know the answer to when they see it. Popular culture (or "pop culture") is "the collection of ideas that are fashionable, in style or commonplace and influence the prevailing culture — often through mass media propagation," according to the dozen-citation summation on Wikipedia. Pop culture is society's mirror; the accumulation of views, opinions, and insights most strongly representative of its people. Flip on the television or the radio, pick up a newspaper or a book, and you're opening a portal to the ever-changing meaning of the words.

Once separated into "high culture" (the culture of ruling social groups) and "low culture" (the vulgar "base" interests of the common people), over time those lines of society's preferences have blurred into one "popular culture," which defines the lives, biases, and the approval or rejection of ideas in the social order.

Popular culture has been called everything from "common culture" to "mass culture," and since World War II everything from clothing to consumption of entertainment has helped attach the tag "commercial culture" to it. Popular culture is also one of the single biggest exports that the U.S. offers the rest of the world. Increasingly, it must be studied and dissected as a key component to American material, economic, and political culture.

Just how powerful a force is popular culture today? The University of California at Berkley founded a "Post World War II American Culture and Literature Database," and prestigious universities Syracuse in New York and Bowling Green State here in Ohio have entire educational departments devoted to popular culture — even offering tracts of study toward master's degrees.

It would be nearly impossible to cover every facet of popular culture. For the purposes of this book, the term is further defined and placed in the context of the region — through the key figures, products, and innovations which have emerged from Northeast Ohio in music, radio, television, print/literature, politics, sports, film, food, art, and invention.

"I think Cleveland's contributions to popular culture speak to the city's own underdog culture. One thing that's true about comedy is that it helps to have an outsider's point of view. If you've always been on the winning team, you're really much less likely to develop a sense of humor about anything. A sense of humor is a weapon, and a response to being downtrodden — which is not to say that Cleveland is downtrodden by any means, but anyone who grew up in Cleveland has always had an underdog feeling about himself or herself. We always feel that way, because of the things that have happened here. The Cuyahoga River catching on fire, the sports teams, the city going into default. These things are not hilarious at the time, but conceptually it's still a funny and defining thing. Cleveland's always been a little bit down on its luck; when you're the butt of a lot of peoples' jokes, it makes you a little bit more combative and want to fight back a little bit."

— *Andy Borowitz, humorist and satirist, The Borowitz Report*

A Brief History of Northeast Ohio through Pop Culture

We already know to some degree what pop culture says about society, but consider some of these questions for a moment: What does the pop culture from a particular region say about that region? How has Northeast Ohio influenced pop culture? How has pop culture from Northeast Ohio influenced society as a whole? How has pop culture from Northeast Ohio influenced pop culture itself, if at all? And how has pop culture from Northeast Ohio influenced Northeast Ohio?

That's a mouthful at best and could easily become a multi-headed hydra of a thesis statement at worst. As The *Plain Dealer* "Minister of Culture" Michael Heaton suggests, boiling it all down to one common denominator or right answer is "like trying to nail mashed potatoes to the wall." He may be right.

But what does the pop culture from Northeast Ohio say about the region? Based on the majority of successes coming from here in the early 20th century and through the 70s, it says that Northeast Ohio was a vibrant, industrial mecca. When Cleveland, the Cuyahoga County seat, was the fifth largest city in the country, attention was focused on the region in a way that it isn't today. When you consider the size of the region and its innovative spirit percolating and sustaining people during those turbulent early 20th century times, it is no wonder that so much of Northeast Ohio's contribution points to that time period.

Indeed across the country, innovation and great entertainment carried Americans through troubled times, a Great Depression, and life during wartime. Yet, today with its population and economy in decline, the Northeast Ohio area has continued to offer unusual and intriguing popular culture, which reflects the trouble and tumult of contemporary times. Who doesn't listen to bands of the 70s like Pere Ubu and Devo, more recent acts like Nine Inch Nails, or watch films like those of Jim Jarmusch, and not feel the frustration, desperation, and decline of the area, even when that's not necessarily the subject of the art itself?

After considering the achievements chronicled here, one could make the argument that Northeast Ohio's contributions to pop culture, regardless of the time period, reveal the region as a sophisticated, complex place that belies the often one-sided, depressed, rustbelt wasteland as it is portrayed to the rest of the country today.

Northeast Ohio is filled with thinking, feeling people. It is expressive, socially conscious, bootstrappingly clever, pioneering, intellectual, diverse and multicultural, spiritually engaged, and affable, though admittedly self-deprecating. Maybe it is even largely cynical in that George Carlin disappointed idealist sort of way. It's also anything but uniform — kind of like those mashed potatoes cited by Michael Heaton.

Northeast Ohio can hang with any other region in the country. Maybe not in terms of sheer volume, but certainly in quality and depth.

"What does the success of popular culture figures from Northeast Ohio say about the region as a whole? What it says is that we do everything the hard way and usually the dark way and mostly with inside jokes, because that's the only way we know, and most of this is Ghoulardi's fault. And it says that even when we win, we never really win, because that's our lot in life, and most of this is the Indians' fault. Devo spent a decade in Akron trying to establish itself as a serious art collective, developed an entirely evolved philosophy of human existence, then scored a top-20 hit, and is remembered ever thereafter as a "one-hit wonder." Rita Dove won a Pulitzer Prize, served as U.S. Poet Laureate, and continues to have to fight those who pigeonhole her by her race and gender — the 'black woman poet.' Jim Jarmusch is one of the most respected makers of contemporary film, but only by other likeminded filmmakers; because his entire bleak monochrome aesthetic is built on his Akron upbringing and because he'll never give it up, he'll never break free. Robert Quine left Akron and almost immediately defined Lou Reed when he most needed definition and helped deliver Tom Waits from the piano bar and entirely delivered Richard Hell and the Voidoids from their own musical shortcomings, and played beautiful amazing music with Matthew Sweet and Brian Eno and John Zorn and then turned 61 and, obscure, committed suicide. I don't care how hard we try (and we try harder than anybody) or how good we get (and we're as good as anybody) the rest of the world will never understand us or give us our due. Not bitter. Just sayin.' The most important thing it says about us is that we keep trying."

— David Giffels, Author, All the Way Home

"Our pop culture says diversity! I believe that's because there are so many nationalities in Northern Ohio, and that naturally affects and influences every part of our popular culture — especially musically. Just look at how different the musicians are from this area: The Raspberries with Eric Carmen. The James Gang with Joe Walsh. Tracy Chapman. Devo. David Allan Coe. Bone Thugs -N- Harmony, just to name a few. Then there are the Rock Hall inductees: Bobby Womack. The O'Jays. Chrissie Hynde. You just can't get much more diverse than that list!"

— Deanna Adams, author,
Rock and Roll and the
Cleveland Connection

Broadcasting: Radio & Television

Radio and television are perhaps the two largest conduits of popular culture, and the reason is simple: proliferation. Both technologies are so incredibly common in American society that anything delivered through either of these mechanisms reaches a gigantic audience and helps forge and create a collective consciousness among Americans. As of 2001, United States Census Bureau and CIA World Factbook statistics, when combined, put the number of televisions per person in the U.S. at "slightly less than one per person" and the number of televisions per household in the U.S. "slightly more than two per household." Those numbers remain fairly accurate today.

Given the automotive culture in the country, the number of radios per person and household appear even greater. A recent study by *Experian Automotive* reveals that there are some 2.28 vehicles per U.S. household, nearly all of them featuring an AM/FM stereo radio as a standard feature. Radios have a decidedly greater stronghold on our society, especially when one considers that *Experian's* statistics don't even cover the number of radios in the home.

Staggering numbers, right? Wait. It gets better: now consider that the Federal Communications Commission puts the number of active AM- and FM-band radio stations in the United States at over 13,000 and the number of broadcast stations across the country at just under 1,800 — not counting the current cable and satellite stations. Now take another step back and think globally: the *CIA World*

Factbook extrapolates that there are over 44,000 radio stations and 21,500 television stations worldwide. Therefore, any content that is generated for either medium and is delivered to a nationwide or worldwide audience is bound to make an impact.

From the earliest days of both mass media channels, Northeast Ohioans have played a critical role in defining them with memorable talent. In radio, Alan Freed redefined popular culture and revolutionized popular music when he coined the term "rock and roll." (In fact, most of the music chapter of this book wouldn't have even happened if not for the groundbreaking Freed). National radio figure Don Imus used Cleveland for a launching pad to a larger national audience and until recently was seen in dozens of countries all over the world on the NBC suite of channels on cable television.

James Burrows, *Cheers* creator, single-handedly transfigured and modernized the television "sitcom" in the 80s; his contributions continue to inform new television programming seen every day. Jack Paar, Mike Douglas, and Phil Donahue all had a hand in establishing talk-show, tabloid-talk, and news-talk television programming as essential viewing.

These few marquee examples say nothing of other Northeast Ohio natives, such as Drew Carey and Patricia Heaton, who have famously appeared with regularity in a broadcast environment. They have helped create memorable and substantial characters and materials, and in some cases have become something of a brand, thanks to their exposure and popularity.

Here is a healthy sampling of those people and an overview of their accomplishments:

Avery Brooks:

An accomplished stage and television actor, Brooks attended Oberlin College before completing his studies at Rutgers University (he was the first African American to earn a Master of Fine Arts degree in acting and directing from Rutgers). Brooks is identified by most for his television roles as "Captain Benjamin Sisko" on the sci-fi television series, *Star Trek: Deep Space Nine* and as "Hawk" in the police/crime drama, *Spenser: For Hire*. Brooks also played the pivotal role of "Dr. Bob Sweeny" in the politically charged dramatic film, *American History X*. He returned to Oberlin College recently to perform in a stage production of Arthur Miller's *Death of a Salesman*.

James Burrows:

This Oberlin College graduate is perhaps best known as the producer and creator of the NBC comedy series, *Cheers*, but he has profoundly shaped the television sitcom over four decades. Without his directorial expertise, *The Mary Tyler Moore Show, The Bob Newhart Show, Laverne & Shirley, Taxi, Wings, Frasier, NewsRadio, 3rd Rock from the Sun, Dharma & Greg, Will & Grace, Two and a Half Men*, and a handful of other beloved sitcoms would not have existed in quite the same way. Burrows has been nominated for 15 Directors Guild of America awards during his career. And with the exception of 1987, Burrows has also been nominated for an Emmy Award every year since 1980.

Drew Carey:

One of Cleveland's archetypal "Everymans," Carey is best known as a stand-up comedian, actor, writer, and game show host, and one of Cleveland's

Drew Carey prepares to address students at a Cleveland State University commencement during the 90s. *(Photo by William Rieter)*

champions and cheerleaders. Raised in the Old Brooklyn neighborhood and a Kent State University attendee, the hardcore Cleveland sports fan served in the U.S. Marines before making a name for himself as a stand-up comic. His popularity on the comedy club circuit led to his own ABC sitcom, *The Drew Carey Show*, which ran for nine years and more than 233 episodes. He also hosted the U.S. version of *Whose Line Is It Anyway?* Carey also penned the autobiography *Dirty Jokes and Beer: Stories of the Unrefined*, and most recently grabbed the long skinny microphone from broadcasting icon Bob Barker to host the game show *The Price is Right* on CBS. In more recent years, Carey has also turned to photography, philanthropy, and political activism, the latter through a series of internet micro-documentary programs called *The Drew Carey Project* on the site www.reason.tv.

Bud Collins:

Born in Lima, this Berea High School and Baldwin-Wallace College graduate is best known as a tennis analyst for the ESPN, CBS, and NBC television networks. Collins's color commentary for the U.S. Open, French Open, Australian Open, and Wimbledon tournaments over the last four decades has become legendary. Aside from being a professional broadcaster, Collins was also a modestly successful tennis pro and coach. His most famous tennis student was the notorious political activist Abbie Hoffman.

Tim Conway:

An Emmy award-winner, Conway was born in Willoughby and grew up in Chagrin Falls, graduating from Bowling Green State University. Conway worked with the late-night legendary television host Ernie "Ghoulardi" Anderson on the *Ghoulardi* show on Cleveland's then-CBS affiliate WJW-TV. Conway also recorded a comedy album with Anderson, and appeared on TV in Cleveland on late night shows *Hoolihan And Big Chuck* and *Big Chuck and Lil' John* with fellow Ghoulardi alum "Big Chuck" Schodowski. Conway went on to star in two of television's most famous and formative comedy shows, *McHale's Navy* and *The Carol Burnett Show*. He's also been blamed by some, at least in part, for the slew of anti-Cleveland jokes that have been made on television throughout the years.

Phil Donahue:

The Cleveland native and broadcast star, along with fellow natives/peers Jack Paar and Mike Douglas, truly defined the talk show, tabloid-talk-, and news-talk television program formats so prevalent in today's

Phil Donahue helped revolutionize television and was wildly successful as a career interviewer and interrogator for the small screen. *(Photo by J. Bach)*

popular culture. He has hosted some 7,000 one-hour segments of television. A St. Edward High School grad, Donahue launched his career right here in Ohio with the *Donahue* program. He won a staggering 20 Daytime Emmy Awards and a George Foster Peabody Broadcasting Journalism Award during his five-decade television career, one that ended with a short-lived MSNBC cable news program. His tenure at MSNBC ended with his sharp criticism of the Iraq War that began in March 2003. He channeled his dissent into a documentary film project/collaboration with filmmaker Ellen Spiro called *Body of War*, which won a 2007 National Board of Review Award for Best Documentary.

Hugh Downs:

Born in Akron and cultured in Lima, Downs is best known as the mouthpiece and lead broadcaster for the ABC television news "magazine" *20/20*, a competitor to the long-running CBS program *60 Minutes* and archetype for the NBC news program *Dateline NBC*. Downs officially became a television personality in 1957 when he joined the NBC late night talk show *The Tonight Show* as announcer and wingman

"With the exception of Chicago, Cleveland has had ... so much success in comedy and writers and comedians over the last 40 years. And a lot of that, I think, you have to attribute to the city's attitude, struggles and underdog/outsider status which seems like the perfect crucible or Petri dish to create a comedian."

— Andy Borowitz, humorist and satirist, The Borowitz Report

to fellow Northeast Ohio native Jack Paar. He continued in that role, and occasionally hosted the show after Paar left, until Johnny Carson took over as host in 1962. A published music composer, Downs also hosted the *Live from Lincoln Center* musical program on public television. He was also host of *The Today Show* on NBC.

Mike Douglas:

The Chicago-born variety show host and television personality launched his ubiquitous *Mike Douglas Show* in Cleveland at NBC affiliate television station WKYC-TV (identified by call letters KYW at the time). His subsequent Emmy Award-winning show, which later moved from Cleveland to Philadelphia, featured guests John Lennon, Yoko Ono, Barbra Streisand, Aretha Franklin, President Richard Nixon, among many others.

Robert Guillaume:

The stage and television actor joined Karamu Players (now known as Karamu House) in Cleveland after leaving college and cut his acting teeth here. Best known for his role as "Benson DuBois" on the television series *Soap* (and its spin-off *Benson*), Guillaume also appeared in the popular shows *Good Times*, *The Jeffersons*, and *The Fresh Prince of Bel-Air*, the latter created by another one-time Clevelander, Andy Borowitz. Guillaume won Emmys for his work on *Soap* and *Benson*; he's the only African-American actor to win the Lead Comedy Actor Emmy. He's also the voice of "Rafiki" the mandrill in the Walt Disney animated feature, *The Lion King*.

Amiable TV talk-show host Mike Douglas had a knack for making his guests feel comfortable in front of the TV camera. *(Cleveland* Press *Collection of the Cleveland State University Libraries)*

Arsenio Hall:

The actor and comedian was born in Cleveland and schooled in Warrensville Heights. While he had some limited success in film, most notably with friend Eddie Murphy's comedy *Coming to America*, he is best known as the host of the syndicated late-night television show, *The Arsenio Hall Show*. While the show never rivaled the popularity of *The Tonight Show* (then hosted by Jay Leno), Hall did score a coup with political overtones when then-Arkansas governor and presidential candidate Bill Clinton was a guest in summer 1992. Clinton delivered a version of Elvis Presley's hit "Heartbreak Hotel" on the saxophone; some say that Clinton's appearance on Hall's show led to his election later that year.

Jack Hanrahan:

The Cleveland native and comedic writer is often identified as the catalyst of all the Cleveland jokes (for good and ill) that emerged during the city's dark period. He was a writer for the television shows *Get Smart, Rowan & Martin's Laugh-In, The Sonny and Cher Comedy Hour,* as well as several dramatic shows. Hanrahan crafted regular put-downs of Cleveland on *Laugh-In* and gave his Flying Fickle Finger of Fate Award to the city with jokes like "Attention Cleveland: Your Lake Just Died" and "Attention Cleveland: Your River is on Fire." As a result, he is credited with launching the popularity of the Cleveland jokes to which we have become accustomed. Other comedians (even local hero Tim Conway, in both local and national venues) followed suit to some degree.

Steve Harvey:

A multiple NAACP Image Award winner, Broderick Steven "Steve" Harvey was born in West Virginia but moved to Cleveland early on and was a graduate of Glenville High School. The stand-up comic, actor, and broadcaster was a long-time host of the late-night television variety show *It's Showtime at the Apollo*. He helmed the WB network sitcom *The Steve Harvey Show,* and was one of four comedians featured in the Spike Lee film, *The Original Kings of Comedy* which launched the careers of D.L. Hughley, Cedric the Entertainer, and Bernie Mac. Harvey served as emcee in the film. Currently, he is the radio host of the nationally syndicated *The Steve Harvey Morning Show.*

Patricia Heaton:

The two-time Emmy Award winning actress from Bay Village is best known as "Debra Barone," the wife of Ray Romano's "Ray Barone" character, on the CBS sitcom *Everybody Loves Raymond.* She graduated from Ohio State in 1980 with a B.A. in drama and appeared on stage and in motion pictures after graduation. She's turned up most often on television, in

"What does the success of popular culture figures from Northeast Ohio say about the region? I think the down-to-earth, hang-dog, blue-collar, sometimes self-esteem-deficient zeitgeist *so prevalent here produces people with a solid sense of* themselves. *If your ego can take the battering in Cleveland — from poor economics, from losing sports teams, or even just the [freaking] seven-month winters it gives you — you can probably make it in New York or Los Angeles or* Darfur. *This place motivates people to get out and succeed or it kills them. People like Drew Carey and my sister have an* Everyman *appeal — the same way that Johnny Carson had Nebraska as his roots that made him appeal to the man on the street. So what does* that *say about the region? It either makes you or* breaks *you."*

— Michael Heaton,
Plain Dealer *columnist and "Minister of Culture"*

shows including *Matlock, Party of Five*, and *The King of Queens*. She's also the voice of the lunch lady in the animated series *Danny Phantom*. Heaton and husband, actor David Hunt, launched a production company in 2001 called FourBoys Productions (named for their four sons), and together they shaped the documentary film *The Bituminous Coal Queens of Pennsylvania*. Heaton is the daughter of legendary sports journalist Chuck Heaton and sister of the Cleveland *Plain Dealer* "Minister of Culture" Michael Heaton. She still maintains a home in Bay Village and is often spotted around her hometown during the holidays.

Don Imus:

The controversial radio broadcaster and television personality was a one-time North Olmsted resident who did a couple stints on Cleveland talk radio at WGAR and WHK. He wasn't here for long either time: he commuted between Cleveland and New York City. His WHK show is considered something of a rebound before Imus returned to New York City. Best known as a broadcaster at New York's WNBC, also one-time home to fellow "shock jock" Howard Stern, Imus's *Imus in the Morning* radio program was simulcast on the cable television networks CNBC and MSNBC.

Don Novello:

Best known as "Father Guido Sarducci" on the NBC late-night sketch comedy show *Saturday Night Live*, the actor-director and stand-up comedian was born in Lorain. Novello's Sarducci character made many crossovers from *SNL*, appearing on *Married...with Children, It's Garry Shandling's Show*, and the cult classic 80s comedy *Square Pegs*. He also reprised the role on the Air America syndicated radio network, working with fellow SNL alum/writer (now U.S. Senator) Al Franken. Novello produced the Toronto-based comedy show *SCTV*, featuring John Candy, Catherine O'Hara, and Martin Short. Novello also had a non-Sarducci role in the film, *Godfather: Part III*.

Jack Paar:

Born in Canton, Paar is best known as host of the NBC late night television program, *The Tonight Show*, which he hosted alongside announcer Hugh Downs. Paar scored his big break as a stand-up comedian on *The Ed Sullivan Show* and as a substitute host for the legendary comedian and vaudeville icon Jack Benny on Benny's radio program. Paar courted controversy with a few notable moments: his 1959 interview with Cuban leader Fidel Castro, a live broadcast from Berlin during the construction of the Berlin Wall in the early 60s, and a spat with newspaper columnist Walter Winchell, which marked a shift in America's media power from print to television. He also introduced the Beatles to a prime time nationwide television audience in January 1964 — a whole month before the British pop act's three consecutive appearances on *The Ed Sullivan Show*, widely accepted as a "milestone" in pop culture.

Al Roker:

Locals will recognize Albert Lincoln Roker, Jr. from his early days as weather anchor and news personality at Cleveland NBC television affiliate WKYC. The New Yorker made his return to his home state and eventually landed as lead weather anchor on the nationally seen *Today Show* on NBC. Roker has experimented with hard news reporting on NBC's cable station,

MSNBC, and he will co-host a new morning program on cable television's The Weather Channel called *Wake Up with Al*. Roker is a cousin to late actress Roxie Roker (who portrayed "Helen Willis" on the hit sitcom *The Jeffersons*) and her son, rock star Lenny Kravitz. Roker has also hosted programs on cable's Food Network (*Roker on the Road, Tricked-out Tailgating*) and penned/co-authored several books, including *Al Roker's Big Bad Book of Barbecue*.

Tim Russert:

The Washington Bureau Chief of NBC News and longest-tenured moderator of the televised political roundtable/forum *Meet the Press*, Russert was a Buffalo, New York, native who studied in Cleveland. He received his undergraduate degree at John Carroll University and graduated with honors from Cleveland State University's Cleveland-Marshall College of Law in the mid-70s. Russert is often credited with coining the political phrase/terminology "red state" and "blue state" in reference to a state's political leaning. He also predicted elections and tracked Electoral College votes on a white board during televised coverage of the 2000 Presidential election. *Time* magazine named Russert "one of the 100 most influential people" in the world in 2008. He also moderated a number of important political debates; his co-moderating of the Democratic presidential candidate debate between Senator Hillary Clinton and then Senator Barack Obama at Cleveland State University was his last.

John Carroll and Cleveland State alum Tim Russert addresses the crowd during the 2008 Democratic Presidential Debate at the Cleveland State University Wolstein Center. *(Photo by Wiliam Rieter)*

Molly Shannon:

Another *Saturday Night Live* alum, Shannon grew up in Shaker Heights and attended Hawken School in Gates Mills. Best known for her character "Mary Katherine Gallagher" on *SNL*, Shannon's role as a painfully manic, unpopular Catholic school girl, void of social grace, was popular enough to merit theatrical treatment in the major motion picture, *Superstar*. Shannon left *SNL* after a six-plus year run, leaving a string of hysterical impersonations behind her, including those of Elizabeth Taylor, Brooke Shields, Courtney Love, Tori Amos, and Liza Minelli. She has appeared in fellow Shaker Heights native David Wain's film *Wet Hot American Summer*, and the SNL spinoff film *A Night at the Roxbury*, as well as on the television shows *Will & Grace* and *In Living Color*.

George Stephanopoulos:

The former political adviser and current broadcaster spent part of his childhood

"I'm a Westsider and my uncle served in World War II. I remember going to Kamm's Corners, sticking my hand out with a 'V for victory' sign like Winston Churchill did. [Cleveland] is the place where a little boy nicknamed Philly began to wonder about the world and climbed a tree at Mrs. Gallagher's house on West 65th and Madison [so he could] see the Terminal Tower . . . from the fourth or fifth limb. You don't forget these things . . . they all inform your future."

— Phil Donahue, Talk show pioneer

in Cleveland and was graduated from Orange High School. He is best known as a critical cog on President Bill Clinton's two campaigns with fellow politicos David Wilhelm and James Carville. He left the White house in 1996 after four years there and went on to become a political analyst for the ABC News network. There Stephanopoulos ultimately inherited the pundit's chair vacated by legendary broadcaster David Brinkley on the Sunday television magazine, *This Week*. Stephanopoulos was the inspiration for the "Henry Burton" character in the novel and film *Primary Colors*. He's also said to have inspired character "Lewis Rothchild" in the Rob Reiner film *The American President* and "Sam Seaborn" in the Aaron Sorkin presidential television drama, *The West Wing*. His memoir All Too Human: *A Political Education* was a *New York Times Best Seller*.

David Wain:

Born in Shaker Heights, Wain attended New York University film school and is best known for his work with stand-up/sketch comedy group "The State." The MTV cable network program with fellow comic writers Michael Ian Black and Michael Showalter lasted three seasons. The three of them eventually formed the cult comedy group "Stella," which was featured on Comedy Central. Wain made his Hollywood directorial debut with the film *Wet Hot American Summer*, a *Meatballs*-like spoof starring Black, Janeane Garofalo, David Hyde Pierce, Paul Rudd, and fellow Shaker Heights pal Molly Shannon. He has most recently appeared as a guest commentator on the VH1 cable show, *Best Week Ever*.

Did You Know? **The NBC television sitcom *30 Rock* features a character from Cleveland, and jokes about the city are regularly featured in the show. An episode from the first season of the show is titled "Cleveland," with some of the storyline taking place there.**

Actress Patricia Heaton was once a spokeswoman for Pantene hair care products.

The auditorium of Shawnee High School in Lima is named after broadcaster and Akron native Hugh Downs.

Martin Savidge, the anchor, reporter, and award-winning journalist worked at then-CBS Cleveland affiliate WJW-TV before stints with NBC and the cable news network CNN. Savidge now reports on the public television program *Worldfocus.*

WJW-TV reporter Martin Savidge interviews Charlie Sheen (a.k.a. pitcher Rick "Wild Thing" Vaughn) during a news segment. *(Photo by Janet Macoska)*

Ed Helms, a correspondent on the Comedy Central cable show *The Daily Show with Jon Stewart,* went to Oberlin College. He's best known as "Andy Bernard" on the NBC sitcom ***The Office*** and recently appeared in the Hollywood smash film, *The Hangover.*

Sports talk show hosts Chris Rose from Fox's *The Best Damn Sports Show Ever* and Mike Golic of ESPN's *Mike & Mike In the Morning* are both from the Cleveland area.

Sportscaster/Clevelander Vince Cellini, best known for his coverage on the cable networks CNN and the Golf Channel, got his start on CBS Cleveland affiliate WJW-TV. He is a College of Wooster grad.

Kelly O'Donnell, the NBC political reporter, shared screen time with former colleague and fellow journalist Martin Savidge at what was then CBS Cleveland affiliate WJW-TV.

After Imani Hakim studied at Cleveland's Karamu House, the child actress went on to star as "Tonya Rock" in the television sitcom *Everybody Hates Chris.*

Clevelander Greg Morris played the role of "Barney Collier" in the television series *Mission: Impossible.* He also had supporting roles in the shows *The Jeffersons, What's Happening, and Vega$.*

Actress Kate Mulgrew, best known for her role as "Kathryn Janeway" on the *Star Trek: Voyager* series, resides in Cleveland and is married to current Cuyahoga County Commissioner, Youngstown-born Tim Hagan.

In the animated TV series *Family Guy,* the name of the elementary school in Quahog, Rhode Island — where the show is set — is called Martin Mull Elementary School.

Diana Hyland (nee Gertner) of Cleveland Heights was the wife and mother in the 70s television show *Eight is Enough.*

Northeast Ohio native Brian Stepanek plays the role of "Arwin Hawkhauser" in the popular Disney Channel sitcom, *The Suite Life of Zack & Cody.*

Ed O'Neill, best known as the all-purpose character "Al Bundy" from the television series *Married with Children,* is from Youngstown.

In 2002 Drew Carey hired the Cleveland Pops Orchestra to record three tunes, including "Cleveland Rocks," for use on *The Drew Carey Show.*

Drew Carey is currently producing a new television show with the working title *Drew Carey Saves Cleveland.* The show is intended to be nationally syndicated.

Filmmaking Clevelanders Joe and Anthony Russo, who brought the film *Welcome to Collinwood* to the big screen with stars George Clooney, William H. Macy, Sam Rockwell, and director Steven Soderbergh, were also responsible for launching the cultish television sitcom *Arrested Development.*

Visual Art

Visual art from Northeast Ohio may not always match the quantity, exclusivity, or elitism of that found in other larger cities in the United States, but its depth, variety, and impact has nonetheless been impressive and influential. The broad imagination and emotive qualities of pop and comic art, in particular, seem to have thrived in the region and then spread broadly across the country. But the diversity within that framework is also extraordinary.

On one end of the spectrum, the success of the American Greetings company and its ability to tap sentimentality and commercial marketing makes it one of the most influential and longstanding art collectives in the entire country. On the flip side, the raw, unfiltered id and alternative artistry of artists like R. Crumb, Derf, Harvey Pekar, and Derek Hess shows a darker, edgier side to the region and its struggles over the years. In between those two bookends, one finds some of the most successful comic art ever to grace the newspaper "funny pages." Ziggy, Funky Winkerbean, Crankshaft, Calvin & Hobbes, and the comic book legend Superman have all come from Northeast Ohio.

And this says nothing of the influence industrial artist/designer and 2006 National Medal of Arts award winner Viktor Schreckengost has had over the years.

American Greetings:

The Brooklyn-based greeting card company, the world's largest, just recently celebrated its 100th birthday. AG is responsible for introducing many characters into the pop culture lexicon, including Tom Wilson's *Ziggy*, *Strawberry Shortcake*, *Care Bears*, *Hollie Hobbie*, and *The Get-Along Gang*. AG's characters have gone on to successful runs as syndicated comic strips, animated television series, and successful toy and product lines directed at children. The American Greetings Properties division, formerly knowns as Those Characters from Cleveland, holds the licensing rights to these and other characters, including those in Viacom's cable Nickelodeon stable. AG has launched the careers of Wilson and underground comics artist Robert "R." Crumb.

Tom Batiuk:

The Akron native and Medina resident created the broadly syndicated comic strip *Funky Winkerbean* after graduating from Kent State University with a degree in painting. *Winkerbean's* tenure has spanned three decades and has more recently turned a corner into more serious social commentary, a bold move for the "funny pages." Batiuk has tackled topics ranging from Intelligent Design to cancer; one of the strip's main characters, "Lisa Moore," lost her life to the disease. Batiuk and Kent State pal Chuck Ayers are also responsible for *Crankshaft*. This equally popular strip features vignettes and glimpses into a cantankerous schoolbus-driving senior who lives with his daughter.

John "Derf" Backderf:

The alternative/underground comic artist spent formative years in Richfield and attended school with serial killer Jeffrey Dahmer. This led to his creation of the Eisner Award-nominated comic book, *My Friend Dahmer*. Derf's nervous sketches and "cranky rants" started running in the *Cleveland Edition* newspaper in 1990, but ultimately led to national syndication in alternative weekly news tabloids across the country. Derf shares a Pulitzer Prize with the newsroom staff of the Akron *Beacon Journal*, of which he was a part in 1995. His work has also graced a range of divergent media outlets including *The Wall Street Journal* and *Playboy*. His other Eisner-nominated graphic novel *Trashed* will continue as a

"On the national level, Harvey Pekar and [John Backderf] 'Derf' are prime examples of success and impact on a national level, without ever treading very far away. Derf is syndicated all over the country. If you pick up the [alternative newspaper] weeklies, Derf's The City *is probably in there. Harvey did what he did here and* American Splendor *was all over the place! I think it says that the art* manifests *itself to some degree in a place like this. And that says to anyone that 'it can happen here' and that should be a great motivator."*

— *Derek Hess, Artist and Co-Author,* Please God Save Us

"I remember having Bob [R.] Crumb over [to our house]. My dad gave him one of his first jobs at American Greetings. They would be playing jazz together while I was drawing pictures on the floor; it was truly a Bohemian experience. I grew up in a great atmosphere and in a great town and I know it. Not all places are the same; not all of them are created equal, or have the same character as Cleveland had or has. It's a rare, unique place and I loved growing up there. From the imaginative open-mindedness *there, to the tolerance and camaraderie among the people . . . and creatively, in my mind, Cleveland is one of the country's most creative resources. Yes, surely this life experience of mine informs* Ziggy *and who he is. He's a Midwesterner and the perfect counterpart to [Charles Schultz's]* Peanuts, *kids who are completely adult in their reasoning. Ziggy is an adult who never forgot the kid he used to be . . . and he approaches life with one foot squarely in his childhood."*

— Tom Wilson, comic strip artist, Ziggy

"webcomic," a semi-biographical, Internet-only comic strip detailing his life and times as a garbage man.

Brian Michael Bendis:

The writer and erstwhile artist was born in Cleveland and is credited with revitalizing the Marvel Comics *Avengers, Daredevil,* and *Spider-Man.* He has worked with Todd McFarlane's Image Comics group, a publishing house best known for the *Spawn* comic book series. Bendis has won a number of Eisner Awards and others for the stark, gothic, and almost film noir-like quality of his storyboards and art. Bendis also dabbled in the animation "reboot" of *Spider-Man* as a television series, but the success of the Tobey Maguire film released around the same time had a hand in undoing that project.

David Brown:

The Cleveland native and artist is credited with founding the Actualism art movement. Actualism art creates the perception of three-dimensional movement from a solid piece of artwork. It produces one of the more unusual eye tricks and optical illusions in visual art.

Robert "R." Crumb:

The artist and founder of the underground comics movement got his start in Cleveland at American Greetings, but he took a left turn into the subversive world of edgy visuals and satire during the course of his career. His characters, including "Fritz the Cat," "Devil Girl," and the "Keep On Truckin,'" are synonymous with the late 60s and early 70s when they were at their peak of popularity. Crumb contributed to independent Zap Comix in the 60s and is responsible for album cover artwork for Big Brother and the Holding Company. Crumb has collaborated with friend Tom Wilson, Harvey Pekar (*American Splendor*), and poet and novelist Charles Bukowski.

Derek Hess:

The Cleveland-based artist is best known for his work on rock and roll posters; it is largely done with acrylic paint, pen and ink, and screen printing. His poster work is often stark, ironic, and edgy. Along with several other artists across the country, he has elevated the "concert flyer advertisement" for indie, punk, and hard rock shows to a new level of high art. His early original prints promoting concerts

Cleveland artist Derek Hess (right) poses with writer/ collaborator Kent Smith. ***(Peter Chakerian collection)***

are highly sought after by collectors. Hess has his own clothing line that features his art (*Strhess Clothing*) and just recently completed a provocative political graphic novel with Cleveland writer/politician Kent Smith called *Please God Save Us*. His work is on display at the Rock and Roll Hall of Fame and Museum and has been featured prominently on album covers, on cable television networks VH1 and MTV, and in *Alternative Press* magazine.

Harvey Pekar:

The Cleveland-born underground comic book writer (and, to a large degree, visual conceptualist) is a quintessential product of his surroundings. He's best known for his *American Splendor* comic series, an autobiographical exploration illustrated by a number of different artists including friend and fellow Clevelander, Robert "R." Crumb. Pekar's comics were quite opposite from what people had come to expect from them; they were dark, edgy, and reality-based. Pekar's work resonated with comic and literary fans in a way different from what others were doing. Pekar's work helped lay the foundation for the popularity of graphic novels and resulted in an *American Splendor* movie, starring Paul Giamatti as Pekar and Hope Davis as his wife, Joyce Brabner.

Viktor Schreckengost:

The Cleveland School of the Arts (now Cleveland Institute of Art) graduate made a profound impact on American culture with his approach to industrial art and design. As prolific as he was as an artist, Schreckengost was equally influential as a teacher; his students went on to make

"Being from here, I suppose you could scientifically study why Northeast Ohio is different. But being here and not being on the East or West coast, I think, kept me and many other artists from getting all caught up in trends and 'what's hip.' Not to be arrogant by any means; it actually keeps us all real, because there's no hype, no 'Next Big Thing.' Everything is down to earth and we can see through a lot of stuff here. The weather, the environment, the changing of seasons, Lake Erie, the historic struggles we've had . . . and our economy hasn't been great in a long while . . . but that all adds up. The fact that people stay here speaks to Northeast Ohio's true grit."

— *Derek Hess, Artist and Co-Author,*
Please God Save Us

major contributions to everything from toy design and manufacturing (for the likes of Fisher-Price) to automotive design for Ford Motor Company, General Motors, and others. Best known in art circles for his Jazz Bowl, Schreckengost's work also graces the Cleveland Metroparks Zoo's pachyderm exhibition. Schreckengost's influence was acknowledged with a 2006 National Medal of Arts award from U.S. President George W. Bush.

Viktor Schreckengost's influence in visual art and industrial design was felt as far away as Fisher-Price, the toy manufacturers. *(Cleveland* Press *Collection of the Cleveland State University Libraries)*

Joe Shuster and Jerry Siegel:

The co-creators of legendary superhero *Superman* grew up in Cleveland and created their durable and enduring American icon in their hometown. The character has endured and reflected decades of political commentary and awareness. Superman is the archetype for all superheroes and as such has defined and influenced comic books, comic art, and many other facets of American popular culture. Superman has been reinterpreted and re-imagined in film, television, and song to reflect the times. Shuster and Siegel struggled to retain some semblance of ownership over their creation and to receive appropriate credit and financial compensation through the years. They did manage to restore their byline and earn a "modest" lifetime pension from DC Comics, which owns the multi-billion-dollar

Jerry Siegel (left) and Joe Shuster launched Superman from Cleveland. *(Photo courtesy of Siegel and Shuster Society)*

character's rights after the hero's creators initially signed them away. That struggle over the rights to Superman was almost as Herculean as the character himself.

Bill Watterson:

The creator of the celebrated *Calvin & Hobbes* comic strip is a Northeast Ohio native who moved back to Chagrin Falls after ending his run of the strip. Watterson's main characters, a wildly imaginative six-year-old boy (Calvin) and his wise-cracking stuffed tiger (Hobbes), graced the pages of newspapers nationwide from 1985-1995. The duo — and the strip's other hysterical characters — carry on in a number of comic strip collections, including *Scientific Progress Goes "Boink"* and *The Essential Calvin & Hobbes.*

Archibald Willard:

The self-taught artist and 86th Ohio Volunteer Infantry member from Bedford painted the famous American oil portrait *The Spirit of '76*, one of the most beloved Revolutionary War-inspired works ever produced. Once a wagon maker's apprentice, Willard created sketches and portraits as he trained. Some of his works actually adorned wagons during that time period. In 1875, he began working on a centennial work that was conceived as a humorous piece. But then his father passed away, and influenced by grief and appreciation, his renowned portrayal of the American Revolutionary War took on a more somber tone. Willard founded the Academy of Art in Cleveland, which famed industrial artist/designer Viktor Schreckengost later attended.

Tom Wilson:

Both Wilson, the creator of the *Ziggy* comic strip character, and his son, Tom Wilson II, have strong ties to the Cleveland area and were residents here for a great many years. Wilson Senior was a creative head manager at American Greetings. He launched the warm, affable, and wise character, with a touch of childhood naïveté, as an American Greetings character, but it became a nationwide sensation as a syndicated comic panel in 1971. His son, Tom Wilson II has been drawing *Ziggy* and carrying the character forward since 1987. He spent most of his formative years in Cleveland.

Tom Wilson's son (also Tom Wilson) carries on the tradition of one of the comic pages' most beloved characters, Ziggy, created in Cleveland.
(Photo courtesy of HCI Books)

Did You Know? **Prominent photojournalist and Cleveland native Margaret Bourke-White's images of downtown Cleveland, World War II, the Korean War, and Mahatma Ghandi almost single-handedly defined photojournalism. Her most impressive works gained worldwide audiences in *Life* magazine and *The New York Times.***

Superman: Born On Krypton... Via Cleveland

"Faster than a speeding bullet. More powerful than a locomotive. Able to leap tall buildings in a single bound." The fighter for "truth, justice and the American way."

The Man of Steel is America's greatest single fictional hero, but what's often lost in the conversation about him is that Superman was not born on the planet Krypton, as the long-running storyline goes. He was born in Cleveland to two fathers, Jerry Siegel and Joe Shuster, during one of the country's darkest eras.

The story, as detailed in *Made in America: Eight Great All-American Creations*, Addison-Wesley (1978), goes something like this:

The year was 1933. The U.S. was in the throes of the Great Depression. Poverty, unemployment, and despair were at an all-time high; food, hope, and money were at an all-time low. People waited in long lines for soup, bread, jobs, and any other assistance offered to them. At this nadir, America truly needed a hero, a "super man," to lift the spirits of its citizens. Just such a character came to Siegel like a dream before sleep.

Reprint of Joe Shuster's iconic cover art for *Action Comics #1* (published June, 1938), featuring the debut of Superman. *(Peter Chakerian collection)*

A fan of science fiction and pulp magazines of the time, Siegel imagined a powerful champion of the weary who had superhuman strength and powers beyond comprehension. The sci-fi works that he and his illustrating pal Shuster had often read carried them through their awkward growing up. When the two discussed Siegel's idea, it wasn't long before they had crafted the first story of Superman, art and all.

The duo had a feeling that Superman would go on to bigger and better things, perhaps as a comic strip in a newspaper. But it was a long six years of rejections and disappointment — some newspaper editors actually thought the Superman character was crude and juvenile — before Siegel and Shuster presented the future Man of Steel to an editor of the *Detective Comics* magazine. He decided that Superman would be a great anchor character for his company's new *Action Comics* title.

At such a desperate time in history, when the duo was offered $130 for exclusive rights to the character, they jumped at the chance for exposure. Despite Superman's becoming a huge triumph, both young

Jerry Siegel (top left) and Joe Shuster (bottom right) created their all-American superhero Superman in Cleveland, then struggled mightily in trying to reverse a bad business decision by underselling the rights to their creation. *(Photos courtesy of Siegel and Shuster Society)*

This is the Glenville home where Superman was born. Doesn't look much like Krypton, but it spawned a multi-billion dollar enterprise and an enduring American pop culture icon.
(Photo by Layne Anderson)

men would come to regret their decision as time passed.

The all-American appeal of the character and the qualities of his mild-mannered alter ego, Clark Kent, started to pull people out of the doldrums of the times. Soon, the Man of Steel was starring in his own comic book, and the public glommed up all things Superman. The publisher, now known as DC Comics, was rolling in the dough.

And while their character was becoming the star of radio serials and television shows, Siegel and Shuster faded into virtual anonymity and a financial miasma, muddled and befuddled by a string of legal struggles in trying to regain the rights to their character.

The duo eventually had their co-creator credits restored , but not until long after their great American character's triumphs had become a nightmarish struggle for the two of them. It is a saga almost as large as the Superman story itself, and is detailed in resources as diverse as master's degree dissertations, the History Channel program *Comic Book Superheroes*, and Marc Tyler Nobleman's book, *Boys of Steel: The Creators of Superman.*

Superman continues today as a reflection of society, a pop culture phenomenon unto himself. He continues to tackle current world events and politics within the context of the storylines in his many comic book titles, and he is still very much a multi-billion dollar brand, despite the changing tastes in the years since his creation. The last "reboot" of the Superman film series, *Superman Returns*, not surprisingly offered a current world view and spin on the ever-popular story.

Superman's legacy also continues in the preservation initiatives laid out by the Siegel and Shuster Society, based in Cleveland, and author/activist Brad Meltzer who, in conjunction with the non-profit AmeriCorps service organization CityYear and Ordinary People Change the World, Inc., helped raise over $100,000 recently to help restore Siegel's childhood home in Glenville where Superman was created.

The subject of countless major motion pictures, live action television shows and cartoons, pop songs, and gads of other mass media signposts, would Five For Fighting, Christopher Reeve, or even *Seinfeld* have had as big an impact without him? Superman stands as the one superhero above all others. Superheroes, as they exist today, may not have assumed their level of cultural importance and significance in our society if not for two wildly imaginative Cleveland kids with one really big idea.

And that's something we can all hang our capes on.

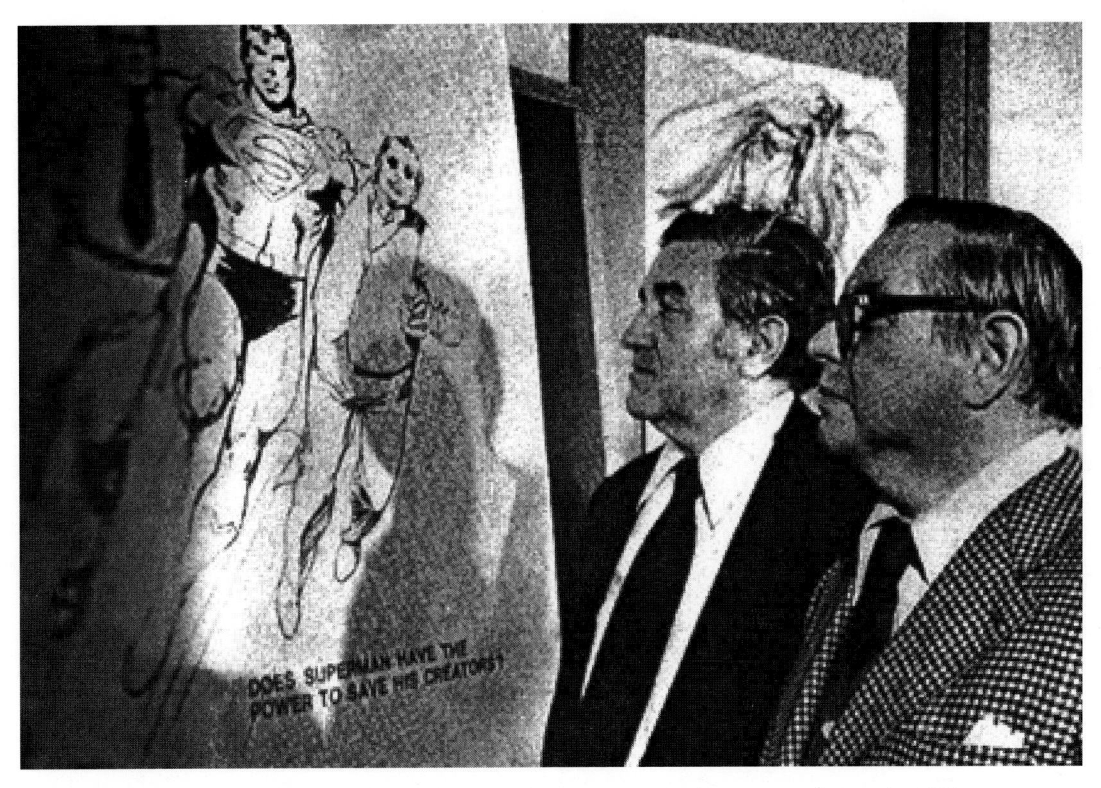

Jerry Siegel (left) and Joe Shuster take in a more modern conception of Superman during the 1970s. *(Photo courtesy of Siegel and Shuster Society)*

Food

Ask the average Northeast Ohio resident to name someone famous for food from these parts and you're likely to hear the name: Michael Symon. The Cleveland-bred Symon is currently the hottest culinary commodity, with his image gracing a handful of television programs on cable's Food Network. But dig a little deeper and you'll find that everything from the modern hamburger and ice cream cone, to the myriad of frozen, prepared, and canned foods, have all come from Northeast Ohio.

Harry Burt:

The Youngstown native re-imagined Iowa store-owner Christian Nelson's chocolate-covered ice cream bar called the Eskimo Pie with a new recipe and the introduction of the stick to the creamy confection. Yes, this happened here in Northeast Ohio. Burt's innovation for convenience and gainful grip led to the invention of the Good Humor ice cream bar (originally called "ice cream suckers") in the early 1920s — with the patents for mass production of the treats officially granted in 1923. The sticks themselves are referred to as "Popsicle sticks" in the pop culture vernacular, but that belies the fact that Frank Epperson (creator of the Popsicle) had co-opted Burt's proprietary ice cream stick idea. Burt ended up settling out of court with Epperson. Today, Good Humor-Breyers is one of the country's largest producers of frozen confections and branded ice cream desserts.

Ettore (Hector) "Chef Boyardee" Boiardi:

Born in Italy, this Cleveland Heights resident became head chef at the Ritz Carlton Hotel in New York at the ripe old age of 17. How's that for ambition? Boiardi came to the Cleveland area after a stint in the Big Apple and launched the Giardion Restaurant (as well as his own Chef Boiardi's), where he sold his own homemade sauces and pastas packaged for takeaway. At first, he actually re-used milk bottles and other containers as carriers for his take-away sauces. Boiardi did quite well at it, so much so that he decided to make a go of the "to go" philosophy of food service. He saw an opportunity in the marketplace and started creating and marketing packaged meals in the early 1930s. It was an overnight sensation, and ultimately a million-dollar business idea. The Chef Boyardee brand carries on today, an acquisition of the global ConAgra food company.

Known to the world as "Chef Boy-ar-Dee," Hector Boiardi came to Cleveland in 1917 from New York City and by the late 1920s had morphed several area restaurants into an in-demand wholesale food business. *(Cleveland* Press *Collection of the Cleveland State University Libraries)*

Clarence A. Crane:

Born in Garrettsville, this candy-making Clevelander launched a new type of hard candy in 1912, responding to the summer decline in sales of his chocolates. Knowing that hot, sticky weather equals gooey, melted chocolate, Crane figured a more solid, longer-lasting candy would be more resistant to the heat and help his sales. He obtained a pharmacist's pill punch machine, punching a hole into his round, hard candy recipe, giving them the appearance of nautical life preservers. He called these tasty treats Life Savers. Crane started out with a small number of flavors, including Pep-o-Mint and Violet (yes, the flower). Crane sold his brilliant idea to a New York candy company for a paltry sum and lost the rights to what is now a multi-billion dollar brand produced by Kraft Foods.

Frank and Charles Menches:

These two Akron brothers invented two of the most famous culinary treats: the hamburger sandwich (1885) and the "cornucopia" ice cream cone (1904). As for the hamburger claim, it has been vigorously debated by several other burger petitioners and cities who also claim to be first. Imagine what your town would be like if every McDonald's, Burger King, Wendy's, Baskin-Robbins, and Dairy Queen suddenly vanished. They also created a caramel-coated popcorn treat similar to confectioner Frederick William Rueckheim's Cracker-Jack. Thanks, Menches, and thanks Akron!

"I don't know that there's one true narrative about what life is like here, or if [lining up successes] helps hold it together as a unified theory . . . Everybody is different and each person really puts his or her own spin on things. I don't think there is any one narrative, but many, and they all say very different things about Cleveland, Northeast Ohio, and the Midwest.."

— *Michael Heaton,*
Plain Dealer *columnist and "Minister of Culture"*

Michael Ruhlman:

The Cleveland-born writer and University School graduate has written a dozen different books on food over the course of his career, many in collaboration with leading chefs. His informative and influential tomes, *The Making of a Chef, The Soul of a Chef, The Reach of a Chef,* and *The French Laundry Cookbook,* have been deemed indispensable by those learning or currently involved in the food industry. Ruhlman appears with regularity on Food Network, PBS, and the Travel Channel as a judge, personality, and culinary expert. His most humorous turn on television was as chef/personality Anthony Bourdain's sidekick on the "Cleveland" episode of the food-travelogue television show, *Anthony Bourdain: No Reservations.* He also wrote briefly about food for *The New York Times.* His latest book, *Ratio: The Simple Codes Behind the Craft of Everyday Cooking,* is already deemed indispensable by chefs and "foodies" alike.

Abraham & Lena Stouffer:

The humble beginnings of a frozen prepared meal empire started in Richfield with the idea of a downtown Cleveland dairy stand in 1922. Stouffer's quickly branched out into the restaurant business by opening a luncheonette in downtown Cleveland. Their chain grew rapidly throughout the region, then expanded to major cities across the country, eventually numbering 65 restaurants. It wasn't long before the public was clamboring for a home version of Stouffer meals. By the

Abraham Stouffer was a pioneer in "fast food" for the home. *(Cleveland* Press *Collection of the Cleveland State University Libraries)*

mid-50s, overwhelmed by the volume of requests for these meals, the Stouffers opened a processing facility to keep up with the demand. The Stouffer brand is now part of Nestle Food Corporation which operates a major facility in suburban Solon.

Michael Symon:

One of the most high-profile food figures in Cleveland, chef/resteranteur Michael Symon has helped draw attention to his hometown with a string of successful and critically acclaimed restaurants, winning the coveted 2009 James Beard Foundation Award for "Best Chef - Midwest" and scoring the title of "The Next Iron Chef" on cable television's Food Network series of the same name. Symon's latest endeavor, a casual American eatery, Bar Symon, opened in the old Swingo's location in Avon Lake in 2009.

Iron Chef Michael Symon emerged from Cleveland to join the ranks of the Food Network elite on cable television. He is pictured here at his restaurant Lola in the East 4th Street entertainment district in Cleveland. *(Photo by Peter Chakerian)*

Did You Know?

The fast food chain Arby's, known for its take on deli sandwiches and referred to at one time as an abbreviation for "America's Roast Beef, Yes Sir!" was founded by Youngstown natives Forrest and Leroy Raffel.

Quaker Oats came to be when four different oats mills merged, including the German Mills American Oatmeal Company in Akron and Quaker Mill Company of Ravenna.

Jerry Greenfield, co-founder of Ben and Jerry's famous Vermont ice cream company, went to Oberlin College.

Inventions and "Firsts" from Northeast Ohio that Impacted Pop Culture

Invention, innovation, and technology have often been the driving force of popular culture. Consider that the 20th century brought the U.S., and the world for that matter, squarely into the automotive age with the establishment of the automobile and relevant technologies to make driving these amazing vehicles more practical, agreeable, and luxurious.

Paving the way for personal freedom (and the byproduct we all see now as "car culture" in America), the automobile is one of the single most important inventions we Americans depend on. But while Detroit, Michigan, is often referred to as the "Motor City" and the catalyst for much of what we see on the road today, the creation of and discoveries by Northeast Ohioans in relation to our lives on the open roads cannot be underestimated.

Consider that Northeast Ohio is responsible for:

- The first electric traffic lights
- The first street lights
- The first balloon (inner tube) tires
- Catalytic cracking of gasoline for use in automobile motors
- The first automobile windshield wipers
- The first American-made "standard gasoline" automobile (1898)
- The first American diesel engine (1913) - Alexander Winton
- The first car driven across the United States
- Being one of the country's main producers of rubber and tires

While Northeast Ohio was a pioneering location for automobile technology, the entire concept of broader "mass" transportation and travel benefited from these "firsts":

* The first electric streetcars
* The first municipal airport (Cleveland Hopkins)
* The first airfield lighting system
* The first air traffic control tower
* The first padded bicycle seat
* The first rapid transit rail service from airport to the downtown city center

Several food firsts happened here in Northeast Ohio as well:

* The first breakfast cereal
* The first decaffeinated coffee
* The first "cornucopia" ice cream cones
* The first caramel popcorn
* The first hamburgers (invented by Akronite Charles Menches, though often disputed)

And if that's not enough to convince you of Northeast Ohio's influence on the American popular culture of today, consider some of these amazing innovations that are now considered requisite modern conveniences and often taken for granted in America:

In modern technology and in home/office conveniences:

* The first whole body scanner and X-ray machine
* The Richter Scale (for measuring the strength of earthquakes)
* Hydroelectric power
* The first wind-powered electric generator (Clevelander Charles F. Brush)
* The first dishwasher
* The first portable electric vacuum cleaner
* The Multigraph Duplicating Machine (precursor to copy machines for printing)
* The first mail delivery (Cleveland was the first to experience this in 1863)
* The first mail delivery uniform

In shopping:

* The first indoor shopping center (The Cleveland Arcade)
* The "father" of shopping mall developers, Ed DeBartolo, Jr. (Youngstown)

In sports:

* The National Football League was established in Canton in 1920 as the American Professional Football Association
* *Monday Night Football* (the first game took place in Cleveland in 1970)
* The first modern golf ball
* The first toy marbles (invented by the first toy manufacturing company, in Akron)

The first museums:

* Home of the Inventors Hall of Fame (Akron)

* Home of the Rock and Roll Hall of Fame and Museum (Cleveland)
* Home of the Pro Football Hall of Fame (Canton)
* Home of the Polka Hall of Fame (Euclid)
* The first public health museum (HealthSpace Cleveland, now part of the Cleveland Museum of Natural History)

And here are some other amazing pop culture "firsts":

* The first official public housing
* The first rock and roll concert — "The Moondog Coronation Ball"
* The second coming of Valentine's Day — Sweetest Day
* The first Labor Day (conceived by Clevelander John Patterson Green, the first African American to hold political office in Cuyahoga County). Launched as a local holiday, it was adopted as a national holiday very shortly after it was established.

And while not technically a Northeast Ohio resident, Thomas Edison was born in Milan, Ohio, in Huron County, ever so slightly west of us. He greatly influenced life across the globe with inventions including the telephone, phonograph, modern electricity, the modern electric light bulb, and motion pictures.

The Cleveland Connection for U.S. President Barack Obama

He's everywhere these days. And why shouldn't he be? Aside from being the President of the United States of America, Barack Obama also happens to be the first African American to assume that role in our nation's history. Yes, he's a Hawaii native, and most recently a Chicago resident, so what does he have to do with Northeast Ohio, exactly? Cleveland had been a pace setter in the quest for racial equity.

Northeast Ohio (particularly Cleveland) is often referred to in relation to the six-day Hough Riots in 1966, but that clearly overshadows the advancement that has taken place for African Americans in the course of the region's history. Consider Barack Obama's election in light of the following list of inestimable "firsts" that happened right here in Northeast Ohio:

* Carl B. Stokes was the first African American elected as mayor of a large U.S. city (Cleveland).

Enjoying a laugh are Congressman Louis Stokes and his brother Carl B. Stokes (right). *(Cleveland Press Collection of the Cleveland State University Libraries)*

* The first African-American newspaper was published by Clevelander William Howard Day in 1852.
* Youngstown journalist Simeon Booker was the first African-American reporter for *The Washington Post.*
* While it's widely accepted that Jackie Robinson was the first African-American Major League Baseball player, Cleveland native Moses Fleetwood Walker played for a Toledo team in the American [Baseball] Association in the 1880s.
* Cleveland Indian Larry Doby was the first African American to play in the American League
* Frank Robinson of the Cleveland Indians was the first African-American manager in Major League Baseball.
* Satchel Paige of the Cleveland Indians was the first African-American pitcher to be inducted into the Baseball Hall of Fame.
* Oberlin College was the first U.S. college to admit students regardless of race, sex, creed, color, orientation.
* Karamu House was the first African-American Cultural Center established in the United States.
* Dorothy Dandridge of Cleveland was the first African-American woman to be nominated for the Academy Award for Best Actress.
* Cleveland native Halle Berry was the first African-American woman to win the Academy Award for Best Actress.
* Lorain native Toni Morrison is the first African American to win the Nobel Prize for Literature.
* Akron native Rita Dove was the first African-American woman named Poet Laureate of the U.S. and also the youngest person in history named to that role.
* East Tech High School graduate Jesse Owens was the first American (African American or otherwise) to win four Olympic gold medals.

Cleveland Indians player/ manager Frank Robinson was the first African American to manage a team in Major League Baseball. In his first at-bat he hit a home run, and that feat was voted by Cleveland fans as the most memorable in Cleveland sports history. *(Cleveland Press Collection of the Cleveland State University Libraries)*

Did You Know? **Kinsman Township native Clarence Darrow was probably the most famous and influential lawyer in the U.S. during the last century. His most famous trials have been recreated in film and stage productions. His "Scopes A Monkey Trial" became the film *Inherit the Wind*, starring Spencer Tracy as Darrow; his "Leopold and Loeb" trial was staged as the play *Compulsion*. A human rights and social justice advocate, Darrow has been portrayed by a number of Hollywood elites including Tracy, Henry Fonda, and Ed Asner.**

Stage & Silver Screen

This is where it gets even more interesting. Northeast Ohio's impact and influence on stage productions and in motion pictures is enormous. From the incomparable comedian/actor Bob Hope and pioneering Halle Berry, to characters like "Freddy Krueger," "Rhett Butler," "Forrest Gump," "The Rat Pack," and the "Wicked Witch of the West," the ties to the region are broad and deep.

Jim Backus:

Born in Cleveland and raised in Bratenahl, Backus was a well-known character and voice actor in film, television, and radio. Best known for his portrayal of wealthy erudite "Thurston Howell III" on *Gilligan's Island*, he was also the voice of *Mr. Magoo*, a similarly rich but hopelessly nearsighted character in the same-titled animated series. Backus also played James Dean's dad in the motion picture *Rebel Without a Cause* and was a key comedic cog in the 1963 ensemble farce *It's a Mad, Mad, Mad, Mad World* which featured a who's who of comedy talent.

Kaye Ballard:

Born Catherine Gloria Balotta in Cleveland, the musical comedienne was a star on Spike Jones's touring revue, before appearing on Broadway and in various television roles. Ballard co-starred in the NBC sitcom, *The Mothers-in-Law*, with Eve Arden, and was a regular role player on *The Doris Day Show* in the early 70s. She also starred opposite Julie Andrews in Rodgers & Hammerstein's *Cinderella*. She also appeared on the *Match Game* show. Ballard's campiest career moment was as a guest host on Jim Henson's *The Muppet Show*, where she and Miss Piggy attempted to upstage each other in "One Note Samba" and sang "Oh Babe What Would You Say" as a duet with big blue monster "Thog."

Halle Berry:

The former beauty queen and fashion model was born in Cleveland and was graduated from Bedford High School. She has arguably been the area's most successful actress to date. She is the first African-American actress to win the Academy Award for Best Actress for her role in the 2001 drama *Monster's Ball*. Berry started her acting career on the prime-time television soap opera *Knots Landing*, but has since gone on to appear in a number of films including the *X-Men* franchise, *Jungle Fever, Bulworth,* and as the Bond Girl "Jinx" in the *Die Another Day* installment of the James Bond 007 series. Berry won an Emmy, a Golden Globe, a

Academy Award winner Halle Berry portrayed fellow Clevelander/actress Dorothy Dandridge on film. *(Photo by Walter Novak)*

Screen Actors Guild Award and NAACP Image Award for her work in *Introducing Dorothy Dandridge*. Ironically, Dandridge was also an actress from Cleveland and was the first African American to be nominated for an Academy Award for Best Actress.

Chris Columbus:

The film director grew up just outside Youngstown and launched his film career with the teen comedy *Adventures in Babysitting*. Columbus has certainly tapped into his "inner child" during his career, lending his talents to the hugely successful 1990 film *Home Alone* and its sequel *Home Alone 2: Lost In New York*, both starring child acting sensation Macaulay Culkin. He went on to film *Stepmom*, and the Robin Williams movies *Mrs. Doubtfire* and *Bicentennial Man*. Columbus adapted the popular Broadway musical *Rent* into a major motion picture and wrote the classic 80s films *Gremlins* and *The Goonies*. He also helmed a pair of *Harry Potter* film adaptations based on the best-selling novels for British author J.K. Rowling.

Wes Craven:

Often referred to as the "Master of Horror," Wesley Earl Craven was born in Cleveland and has gone on to redefine the horror genre of motion pictures in Hollywood and beyond. He is best known as the creator of and director for the infamous, blade-gloved "Freddy Krueger" slasher character featured in the *Nightmare on*

The "Master of Horror" looks on during the filming of *Scream* — the second of his infamous horror film franchises. *(Peter Chakerian collection)*

Elm Street film series. Most horror film directors to emerge after *Elm Street* cite Craven as an influence. Craven himself managed to repeat his 80s success with another film, the mid-90s suspense film *Scream*, and its two sequels, which featured another psychopathic slasher referred to as "Ghostface." His pair of silver screen creepies are among the most recognizable in American cinema, along with *Friday the 13th*'s hockey-masked man "Jason Vorhees" and *Halloween*'s "Michael Myers."

Dorothy Dandridge:

The singer-actress was born in Cleveland in 1922 and went on to become the first African American nominated for an Academy Award for Best Actress.

Cleveland actress Dorothy Dandridge was nominated for an Oscar (Best Actress) for her work in Otto Preminger's 1954 film *Carmen Jones.* *(Peter Chakerian collection)*

Dandridge toured with her sister across the southern U.S. for several years under the moniker The Wonder Children before moving to Hollywood. She went on to make films before hitting the road again with her sister as The Dandridge Sisters and singing in well-known venues including the Cotton Club speakeasy and The Apollo Theater in New York. Dandridge's first on-screen role was in an *Our Gang* short film, better known in pop culture circles as *The Little Rascals.* She was nominated for an Oscar (Best Actress) for her work in Otto Preminger's 1954 film *Carmen Jones*, starring Harry Belafonte and Pearl Bailey.

Ruby Dee:

The Academy Award-nominated actress was born in Cleveland and went on to appear in dozens of films and stage productions. Also a poet, playwright, and activist, Dee (nee Ruby Ann Wallace) earned critical raves for her roles in *A Raisin in the Sun* and *Edge of the City*, both opposite actor Sidney Poitier. At age 83, Dee was nominated for an Academy Award for Best Supporting Actress for her role in the 2007 Denzel Washington film *American Gangster* for which she won the Screen

Actors Guild award. Both she and husband actor-director Ossie Davis shared the 2007 Grammy Award for Best Spoken Word Album with former President Jimmy Carter for their biographical *With Ossie And Ruby: In This Life Together.*

Joe Eszterhas:

The Bainbridge native and former reporter for The *Plain Dealer* was a one-time senior editor for *Rolling Stone* magazine and is best known for his "pulp erotic" screenplays *Showgirls* and *Basic Instinct*, which became major motion pictures. Eszterhas's first produced screenplay was *F.I.S.T.*, a labor union drama set in Cleveland and starring Sylvester Stallone. His edgy writing went on to propel a string of successful films including *Flashdance, Jagged Edge, Jade, Betrayed*, and *Sliver.* His semi-biographical 1997 film, *Telling Lies in America*, is set in Cleveland and was filmed here detailing a Hungarian immigrant's adjustment to life in the United States. In 2004, Eszterhas wrote the spicy-and-scandalous tell-all book *Hollywood Animal* which described various "sexcapades with Hollywood actresses and nasty battles with Hollywood execs." His latest book, *Crossbearer: A Memoir of Faith*, details his spiritual conversion and commitment to family and God in the wake of a hard-fought battle against alcoholism and cancer brought on by years of heavy smoking.

Northeast Ohio native Joe Eszterhas' semi-biographical 1997 film, *Telling Lies in America*, is set in Cleveland and was filmed here. He is pictured here in the Flats in a 1986 photograph. *(Photo by Janet Macoska)*

Angie Everhart:

Born in Akron, this actress and former fashion model graduated from Harvey S. Firestone High School. She graced the covers and pages of *Elle* and *Glamour* magazine before becoming a *Sports Illustrated* swimsuit edition sensation in 1995. She has appeared in several subsequent editions of the annual. Everhart made her film debut in the 1993 action flick *Last Action Hero* starring Arnold Schwarzenegger and went on to star in the horror-comedy *Tales From the Crypt Presents: Bordello of Blood.* At various times during her career, she was linked romantically to radio shock jock Howard Stern, actors Sylvester Stallone and Joe Pesci (she was engaged to both), and to royalty in Prince Andrew, Duke of York, and Prince Albert of Monaco. She was most recently a co-host on the ABC reality show *The Ex-Wives Club.*

Clark Gable:

Nicknamed "The King of Hollywood," the Akron resident and Academy Award-winning actor is best known for portraying the role of "Rhett Butler" in the epic 1939 Civil War film *Gone With the Wind* and

"Frankly, My Dear . . ." Clark Gable was an Akron resident for a time before launching into the Hollywood stratosphere. *(Cleveland* Press *Collection of the Cleveland State University Libraries)*

"Fletcher Christian" in the equally-popular *Mutiny on the Bounty.* A Hollywood heartthrob, Gable lived and worked in Akron for a time before moving to California to earn wide acclaim and success as a motion-picture actor.

Teri Garr:

Terry Ann Garr was born in Lakewood to entertainer parents and attended Magnificat High School in Rocky River. After a career breakthrough performance in Mel Brooks' *Young Frankenstein*, Garr went on to star in a string of successful films in the late 70s including *Close Encounters of the Third Kind, Oh, God!* and *The Black Stallion.* She also appeared with Kent State University attendee Michael Keaton and North Ridgeville native Martin Mull in the 1983 comedy, *Mr. Mom.* Garr was nominated for a Best Supporting Actress Academy Award for her role as Sandy Lester in *Tootsie* (her co-star Jessica Lange won the award). She has also spent her fair share of time on television, most recently in a recurring role as the estranged mom of "Phoebe" on the NBC sitcom, *Friends.*

Lillian Gish:

Born in Springfield, the actress grew up in Massillon and has a street named after her in that hometown. She was a prominent film star of the early 20th century and is best known for her leading role in D. W. Griffith's influential silent film, *The Birth of a Nation.* Gish was nominated for the Academy Award for Best Supporting Actress in 1946 for her work in *Duel in the Sun*; she would receive an Honorary Academy Award some 25 years later. The American Film Institute named the actress #17 of the greatest female film stars of all time. They honored her with a Life Achievement Award in 1984.

Joel Grey:

Born Joel David Katz in Cleveland and schooled in Cleveland Heights, the actor of stage and screen is best known as the "Master of Ceremonies" in the stage and film adaptation of *Cabaret.* Grey has been highly decorated for his work. He has received Tony, Golden Globe, British Academy of Film and Television Arts, and Academy awards. In fact, Grey is one of only nine people who have won both a Tony Award and an Academy Award for the same role. Stage production aficionados will recognize Grey's work in *Chicago* and *Wicked*; younger audiences are likely to recognize him from roles on the television shows *House, Law & Order: Criminal Intent*, and *Alias.*

Tom Hanks:

A two-time Academy Award winner for Best Actor, Thomas "Tom" Jeffrey Hanks interned and got his big break with Cleveland's Great Lakes Theater Festival (GLTF) company, where he made his professional acting debut as "Grumio" in *The Taming of the Shrew.* Hanks appeared in other GLTF productions, including *Two Gentleman of Verona*, which earned him the Cleveland Critics Award for Best Actor. From Cleveland, Hanks went on to New York, then Hollywood, and the rest, as they say, is history. One of the silver screen's most famous actors, Hanks has starred in *Big, Splash, A League of Their Own, Saving Private Ryan, Cast Away*, the *Toy Story* series of animated films, and *The Da Vinci Code*, among others. He won his Best Actor Oscars for *Philadelphia* and, of course, *Forrest Gump* — which also won Best Picture in 1994.

Film legend and Great Lakes Theater Festival alum Tom Hanks addresses a Great Lakes Theater Festival crowd in 1991. *(Photo by Janet Macoska)*

Anne Heche:

The Aurora-born actress won a Daytime Emmy and *Soap Opera Digest* Award for her work on the soap opera *Another World* before branching out into motion pictures. While her personal life and relationships have often overshadowed her acting career, most notably her relationship with comedienne/talk show host Ellen DeGeneres, Heche's career has been a sturdy one. She's been involved in a string of hit films including *Six Days Seven Nights* with Harrison Ford, *Wag the Dog, I Know What You Did Last Summer*, and director Gus Van Sant's "reboot" of the legendary 1960 Alfred Hitchcock film, *Psycho.* Heche has most recently been seen in the ABC television "romatic dramedy" *Men in Trees.*

Hal Holbrook:

Holbrook earned his first paid professional engagement playing the son in *The Man Who Came to Dinner* at the Cain Park Theatre in Cleveland Heights. The Cleveland-born actor (nee Harold Rowe Holbrook, Jr.) knows a thing or two about Mark Twain. The Emmy- and Tony-Award winning actor's calling card is in the performance of the celebrated author once known as Samuel Clemens. His solo stage performance of *Mark Twain Tonight* still tours regularly and, at nearly 75 years old, the "great craftsman of stage and screen" still helms the production himself. He earned his first Academy Award nomination for Best Supporting Actor for *Into the Wild* in 2008.

Bob Hope:

Leslie Townes Hope was the godfather of modern American stand-up comedy, but he was actually born in England and later moved with his family to Cleveland.

Hope's career stretched across comedy, vaudeville, film, stage, and both radio and television. Highly regarded for his work with the United Service Organization (USO) and its collective service to the U.S. military, he supported the group through variety shows and other humanitarian efforts. Hope starred alongside contemporaries Bing Crosby and Doris Day, and with other Hollywood mainstays during a 60-movie career. An avid sports fan, he served as a catalyst for the celebrity "pro-am" golf tournament, The Bob Hope Celebrity Classic. In the 50s, Hope was also part owner of the Cleveland Indians and was guest of honor at the last game the team played in old Cleveland Municipal Stadium.

Bob Hope takes a swing during one of his many golf events. A champion of the USO, this multi-faceted entertainer was also a sports buff who shared ownership of the Cleveland Indians for a time. Although he was born in England, he came into his own in Cleveland. *(Cleveland Press Collection of the Cleveland State University Libraries)*

Terrence Howard:

Though born in Chicago, this critically acclaimed actor spent most of his formative years in Cleveland. Nominated for nearly a dozen awards for his performance in the silver screen drama *Hustle & Flow*, Howard first appeared in the Richard Dreyfus film, *Mr. Holland's Opus*. He would go on to star in two Academy Award-nominated films for Best Picture in 2004, the drama *Crash* and the Ray Charles film *Ray*. His first foray into pop music, a "neo-Soul" album called *Shine Through It* was released in fall 2008. His most recent role came as "Lt. Colonel James 'Rhodey' Rhodes" in the Hollywood blockbuster and Marvel comics adaptation of *Iron Man*.

Jim Jarmusch:

The director and independent filmmaker born in Cuyahoga Falls was quoted in *The New York Times* that "[g]rowing up in Ohio . . . was just planning to get out." A wildly inventive conceptualist, Jarmusch's non-traditional filmmaking has made him something of a counterculture icon himself. Heavily influenced by underground heroes, Jarmusch points to Ghoulardi, Frank Zappa's Mothers of Invention, and beat poets like William S. Burroughs and Jack Kerouac as inspirational during his formative years. He is best known for the films *Coffee and Cigarettes* and *Broken Flowers*, starring Bill Murray. He earned acclaim with his "Far-East philosophical crime" drama *Ghost Dog: The Way of the Samurai* featuring Oscar-winner Forest Whitaker.

Melina Kanakaredes:

The Firestone High School graduate and Akron expat started her acting career as "Eleni Cooper" on *Guiding Light*, a role for which she would earn a Daytime Emmy Award. Her early television roles included stints on *Northern Exposure, The Ben Stiller Show*, and HBO's acclaimed prison drama, *Oz*. Kanakaredes is best known for her role as Dr. Sydney Hansen on the successful NBC drama *Providence* (1999-2002), and is currently co-starring with Gary Sinise on the CBS crime drama *CSI: NY*. She has appeared in the feature films *The Long Kiss Goodnight* starring Samuel L. Jackson and Geena Davis, and *Rounders*, starring Matt Damon and Edward Norton.

Michael Keaton:

Keaton is originally from Coraopolis, Pennsylvania (near Pittsburgh) but he did attend Kent State University as a speech major for a couple years before dropping out and moving back to his hometown. Had he not done so, the actor most recognizable as *Batman* in the Tim Burton-fashioned films might not have landed a gig as a "Flying Zucchini Brother" on the legendary children's television show, *Mister Rogers' Neighborhood*. An 80s film staple, Keaton scored hits with the films *Mr. Mom*, featuring fellow Northeast Ohio expats Martin Mull and Teri Garr, *Johnny Dangerously*, and *Beetlejuice*.

John Lithgow:

The versatile actor of stage and screen spent his formative years as a resident of Akron and Lakewood. Lithgow is best known for his character "Dr. Dick Solomon" on the NBC television sitcom *3rd Rock from the Sun* (1996-2001), but he has won Emmy and Tony awards (and been nominated for two Academy Awards). His most critically acclaimed roles include those in the Bob Fosse film *All That Jazz* and the dramatic films *Terms of Endearment* and *The World According to Garp*. Lithgow has also appeared in the Oscar-nominated films *Kinsey* and *Dreamgirls*. Kids are likely to recognize Lithgow's voice as "Lord Farquaad" from the animated *Shrek* films.

Dean Martin:

One-fifth of the legendary entertainment clan "The Rat Pack" and half of the equally renowned "Martin and Lewis" with comedian Jerry Lewis, Dean Martin was born Dino Crocetti in Steubenville. He first performed on stage at Craig Beach (near Youngstown) and went through a series of stage names including "Kid Crochet" and "Dino Martini." He went on to croon and tell jokes in and around Cleveland before breaking into the larger audience. His biggest record "That's Amore" continues to be one of the most popular recordings in the modern era. Martin's role in the bank heist movie *Oceans Eleven* with fellow Rat packers Frank Sinatra, Sammy Davis, Jr., Peter Lawford, and Joey Bishop is among his most notable.

Dean Martin (second from left, pictured here with crooner Frank Sinatra) spent his formative years in Cleveland and was a member of the Hollywood elite group "The Rat Pack" with Sinatra. ***(Cleveland*** **Press** ***Collection of the Cleveland State University Libraries)***

Burgess Meredith:

Born Oliver Burgess Meredith in Cleveland, the two-time Academy Award-nominee and Tony Award-winner did his share of stage productions during his nearly seven-decade career. He is best known for portraying Rocky Balboa's trainer Mickey Goldmill in the *Rocky* film franchise and "The Penguin" in the 60s campy television series *Batman* starring Adam West and Burt Ward. He was one of only two people to star in four episodes of the original TV series *The Twilight Zone*.

Martin Mull:

Raised in North Ridgeville until he was a teenager, Mull wears many hats. A stand-up comic who also happens to paint and play guitar, he became well known in the Norman Lear soap opera parody *Mary Hartman, Mary Hartman*. He went on to star in several successful box office ventures including *My Bodyguard, Take This Job and Shove It, Mr. Mom, Clue*, and *Jingle All the Way*. He continued in recurring roles on many television series including *Roseanne, The Simpsons, Growing Pains, It's Garry Shandling's Show,* and the Fox animated series, *American Dad.*

Actor Paul Newman (center) poses with Cleveland Indians players Leon Wagner, Chuck Hinton, and Rocky Colavito (clockwise around him). Newman won the Academy Award for Best Actor in *The Color of Money*. *(Cleveland* Press *Collection of the Cleveland State University Libraries)*

Paul Newman:

The renowned movie star was born in Shaker Heights and was proud to call it home, as he did in several interviews during the course of his career. Newman starred in dozens of popular and memorable motion pictures, including *Butch Cassidy and the Sundance Kid* and *The Sting*. Considered a heartthrob by gads of women moviegoers, Newman won a Best Actor Academy Award for his performance in the 1986 Martin Scorsese film *The Color of Money* – in which he co-starred with another Hollywood hunk, Tom Cruise – as a pool-hall hustler. His spirit lives on in his films and in the philanthropic/charitable work done through his popular "Newman's Own" organic food brands.

Laura Paglin:

The Cleveland Heights native moved from Oregon to attend the Cleveland Institute of Music. After earning a master's degree in piano performance, she turned her attentions to another love – filmmaking. Paglin's independent documentary film *No Umbrella – Election Day in the City* was one of 50 films chosen (from over 4000 submissions) to be screened at the Utah-based Sundance Film Festival founded by actor Robert Redford. *No Umbrella* details the breakdown of polling in inner-city Cleveland and the election process failures during the 2004 presidential election.

Ron O'Neal:

The actor and alumnus of Cleveland's Karamu House theatre appeared in roles on television sitcoms *A Different World* and *Living Single*, but is best remembered as "Youngblood Priest" in the blaxploitation film *Super Fly*.

James Pickens, Jr.:

The versatile stage and television actor is a Karamu House alum who also attended Bowling Green State University. Since 2005, he has played the role of Dr. Richard Webber on the ABC drama *Grey's Anatomy* and has been on *The West Wing, Beverly Hills 90210*, and *Roseanne*.

Debra Winger:

Born Mary Debra Winger in Cleveland Heights, the actress is best known for her string of Hollywood successes in the 80s films *Urban Cowboy* (with John Travolta), *Cannery Row, An Officer and a Gentleman* (with Richard Gere), and *Terms of Endearment*. She has been nominated for several awards for her film work.

Sean Young:

The film actress from Cleveland Heights appeared in several popular motion pictures throughout the 80s including *Stripes* with Bill Murray, the science fiction epics *Blade Runner* and *Dune*, the political thriller *No Way Out* with Kevin Costner and in director Oliver Stone's meditation on greed and excess, *Wall Street*. She has since appeared in a number of independent films as well.

Did You Know?

Actor Alan Ruck played "Cameron Frye" in the classic 80s comedy film *Ferris Bueller's Day Off.* He was born in Cleveland and was featured in the films *Speed, Twister* and *Star Trek Generations.* He attended Parma High School.

The Michael J. Fox/Joan Jett film *Light of Day* was filmed at the Euclid Tavern in Cleveland.

Cleveland-born filmmaker Roland West is acknowledged as an early pioneer of film noir cinema. West's work has influenced numerous directors from David Lynch and Quentin Tarantino to Martin Scorsese and Jim Jarmusch.

Tom Hanks fought Arthur "The Fonz" Fonzarelli (Henry Winkler) in an episode of the TV sitcom, *Happy Days.* Hanks would go on to collaborate with another *Happy Days* alum — "Richie Cunningham" (Ron Howard) — on several motion pictures.

Academy Award-winner Tom Hanks has starred in or been intimately involved with 19 different motion pictures grossing over $100 million each at the worldwide box office. That's a career you can bank on.

How's this for a metropolis connection? Actress Anne Heche voices the role of "Lois Lane" in the animated *Superman: Doomsday* feature film.

Former Clevelander Joel Grey is the father of actress Jennifer "Nobody Puts Baby in the Corner!" Grey, the star of the Hollywood blockbuster *Dirty Dancing.*

Bob Hope is a four-time Hollywood Walk-of-Fame star award winner. Only Gene Autry, with five, has been honored more.

Bill Irwin, the highly lauded performance artist, Tony Award-winning actor, and clown is a graduate of Oberlin College. He has appeared in many television and stage productions, and he is credited with the revitalization of circuses during the 70s.

Native Clevelander, Euclid High School grad, and actress, Monica Potter got her start on the soap opera *The Young and The Restless.* She has since appeared in several television shows and the feature films, *Patch Adams, Con Air,* and *Without Limits.*

Theatrical director Julie Taymor is responsible for the look and feel of the explosive Broadway stage sensation *The Lion King.* She is an Oberlin college grad.

Northeast Ohio in the Movies

The influence on motion pictures doesn't end with the Hollywood stars mentioned previously. Check out the number of major motion pictures that have either featured Northeast Ohio as a setting, as a movie set, or in some cases both:

Filmed in Northeast Ohio, Set Elsewhere

A Christmas Story
Air Force One
The Deer Hunter
Double Dragon
Ghost in the Machine
Happy Gilmore
House Arrest
Men in Black
One Trick Pony
Planes, Trains & Automobiles
Proximity
The Rainmaker
The Shawshank Redemption
Traffic
Spider-Man 3
View From the Top
Welcome to Collinwood

Set in Northeast Ohio, Filmed Elsewhere

Almost Famous
Beautiful Ohio
The Battle of Shaker Heights
Detroit Rock City
The Express
F.I.S.T.
Howard the Duck
Light of Day
Major League
Major League II
This is Spinal Tap

Set and Filmed in Northeast Ohio

Against the Ropes
American Splendor
Antwone Fisher
Flash of Genius
The Fortune Cookie
The Kid from Cleveland
More Than a Game
The OH in Ohio
The Rocker
The Shadow Creature
The Soloist
Stranger Than Paradise
Telling Lies in America
Those Lips, Those Eyes

Actors Tom Berenger and Charlie Sheen from the film *Major League* chat with Cleveland Indians outfielder Mel Hall at Cleveland Municipal Stadium in 1988. *(Photo by Janet Macoska)*

The pairing of Joan Jett and Michael J. Fox from the film *Light of Day* (filmed at Cleveland's Euclid Tavern in University Circle) is reprised in this shot from the movie's 1987 premiere party. *(Photo by Janet Macoska)*

This Tremont location gained immortality from its role in *A Christmas Story*; it has since opened as a theme-based museum/gift shop. *(Photo by Layne Anderson)*

The home of the world-famous Cleveland Orchestra played host to some scenes in the film *Air Force One*, starring Harrison Ford. *(Photo by Layne Anderson)*

Did You Know? Writer/director Bob Clark struggled to get *A Christmas Story* made. Clark, who then had been best known for directing the frat-boy comedy *Porky's*, had to agree to a *quid pro quo* of sorts with the movie studio: it agreed to "greenlight" the former if he agreed to write and direct a sequel to the latter.

Print & Literature

Imagination and creativity reign supreme in this category of Northeast Ohioans. They are writers of edgy post-modern fiction, brilliant science fiction, biting political satire, amazing poetry, and many other forms. The variety is staggering.

Dr. Bertice Berry:

A jack-of-all-trades, this award-winning entertainer, author, lecturer, and comedienne holds a Ph.D. in sociology from Kent State University and won the national Comedian of the Year Award four times during the 90s. She has created her own niche, delivering serious societal messages with brilliant comedic effect. Berry also penned the best-selling memoir, *I'm On My Way, But Your Foot Is On My Head*, and a pair of books called *Sckraight from the Ghetto: You Know You're Ghetto If...* and the sequel, *You STILL Ghetto.* She has also written a work of fiction, *Redemption Song*.

Eric Bogosian:

Born in Massachusetts, the Armenian-American actor, playwright, and novelist graduated from Oberlin College before moving to New York City to launch his idiosyncratic career. A strikingly singular stage presence, Bogosian's manic pastiche of dark comedy and social realism has been a guiding force for a whole generation of

Armenian-American actor, playwright, and novelist Eric Bogosian graduated from Oberlin College. Some of his best written works, including *Talk Radio,* are included in the anthology *Essential Bogosian. (Peter Chakerian collection)*

writers. The 1988 Oliver Stone film *Talk Radio* stars Bogosian as Barry Champlain, a radio shock jock who is Rush Limbaugh plus Howard Stern — almost predicting the rise of both broadcasting figures. Part performance artist, part social commentator, all unfiltered id, you can currently find Bogosian portraying Captain Danny Ross on NBC's television series, *Law & Order: Criminal Intent.*

Andy Borowitz:

Borowitz was born in Shaker Heights and graduated magna cum laude from Harvard University, where he served as president of the legendary humor magazine, the *Harvard Lampoon* (famous *Lampoon* alums include William Randolph Hearst, John Updike, George Plimpton, and Conan O'Brien). He created the NBC hit television series *The Fresh Prince of Bel-Air,* which launched the career of actor Will Smith and won Borowitz a NAACP Image Award. A stand-up comedian, satirist, and "humorologist," Borowitz has written for sitcoms *The Facts of Life* and *Square Pegs,* and his work can be found in places as diverse as the Huffington Post website and *The Daily Show with Jon Stewart.* He also offers syndicated scribing on *The Borowitz Report.* A National Public Radio commentator, frequent guest on MSNBC's *Countdown with Keith Olbermann*, and a columnist in the magazines *The New Yorker, Newsweek*, and *Vanity Fair,* Borowitz has also written six books and co-produced the Academy Award-nominated film *Pleasantville*, starring Reese Witherspoon and Tobey Maguire.

Comedian and faux political pundit Andy Borowitz, pictured here with wife/author Olivia Gentile, has mastered nearly all forms of media and won several awards for his work. *(Photo courtesy of Andy Borowitz)*

Dan Chaon:

The author and Cleveland Heights native released two collections of short stories (1996's *Fitting Ends* and 2001's *Among the Missing*) to critical acclaim; the latter was a finalist for a National Book Award and scored high praise from *The New York Times* and the American Library

Association. Chaon made literary waves with the best-selling first novel, 2004's *You Remind Me of Me*— a coming-of-age tale rooted in family dysfunction. He was awarded the 2006 Academy Award in Literature from The American Academy of Arts and Letters. Chaon teaches creative writing at Oberlin College; his *Await Your Reply* was released in 2009.

Hart Crane:

The son of Life Savers creator/candy man Clarence Crane, Harold Hart Crane was born in Garrettsville and moved back and forth between Cleveland and New York City over the course of his short 32-year life. A pioneer of American Modernism and Romanticism, Crane saw the "father of free verse" Walt Whitman as a hero. He has inspired generations of writers, from legendary poets Allen Ginsberg, e.e. cummings, and Jack Kerouac, to playwright Tennessee Williams.

Rita Dove:

The Akron-born writer served as United States Poet Laureate and Consultant to the Library of Congress from 1993-1995. She won the 1987 Pulitzer Prize for Poetry for perhaps her most famous work, *Thomas and Beulah*. Dove's two-tiered collection of poems used the lives of her maternal grandparents as a semi-fictional starting point.

Harlan Ellison:

The Hugo and Nebula award-winning science fiction writer was born in Cleveland and grew up in Painesville. He made several appearances in productions at the Cleveland Play House before making a move to New York City to pursue a writing career. He wrote for the original television series *Route 66, The Man from U.N.C.L.E.*, and sci-fi classics like *The Outer Limits* and *Star Trek*. Many fans credit Ellison's work with launching the modern science fiction movement. Ellison is not shy about defending his concepts and work; he successfully sued to have his name added to the credits of the Arnold Schwarzenegger blockbuster film, *The Terminator*. He claimed that the film's concepts of time travel and indestructible robots were his and lifted by the film's director/screenwriter James Cameron.

Harlan Ellison revolutionized the sci-fi genre in print, film, and television. He created a multimedia juggernaut before such a term even existed. *(Cleveland* Press *Collection of the Cleveland State University Libraries)*

Ian Frazier:

Frazier was born in Cleveland to a Sohio chemist father and "amateur actor" mother. He schooled at Western Reserve Academy in Hudson, before attending Harvard University and cut his humorist/ satirist teeth on staff at the *Harvard Lampoon*. Lauded for his first-person narratives anchored with in-depth research, Frazier's humor cachés *Dating Your Mom* and *Coyote v. Acme* – the latter a notorious mock-legal complaint filed by

Warner Brothers' cartoon character Wile E. Coyote against Acme Products Corp. — are sheer genius. Frazier is best known for his 1989 non-fiction history *Great Plains*, and as a writer/humorist for *The New Yorker.*

James Frey:

While he has delivered forceful literary work, the Cleveland-born writer/producer is probably best known for his on-air run-in with global media diva Oprah Winfrey. She kicked him out of her very influential "Oprah's Book Club" after finding out that his best-selling "memoir" *A Million Little Pieces* was fictionalized to some degree. In May 2009, it was reported by *Vanity Fair* that Winfrey had contacted Frey and made a formal apology for dressing him down in front of a global television audience. The blurring of fiction and non-fiction notwithstanding, Frey's "experiences" during treatment for drug and alcohol addiction at a Minnesota rehabilitation facility drew in millions of readers.

David Giffels:

The Akron native co-authored two books, the 2003 Devo biography *Are We Not Men? We Are Devo!* and the 1998 historical work *Wheels of Fortune: The Story of Rubber in Akron*, before landing his first book that made it to the top of Oprah Winfrey's "Fantastic Summer Reads" list, *All the Way Home: Building a Family in a Falling Down House*. Giffels, an Ohio Associated Press award winner and former Akron *Beacon Journal* columnist, also worked as a National Public Radio commentator and as a writer on the MTV's animated series *Beavis and Butthead.*

William Goldman:

The two-time Academy Award-winning novelist and screenwriter is an Oberlin College graduate. In addition to writing over a dozen books, he has crafted nearly double that number of screenplays, including *The Stepford Wives, The Princess Bride*, and an adaptation of Stephen King's novel *Misery*. Goldman's two Oscars were for Best Original Screenplay for *Butch Cassidy and the Sundance Kid*, which starred Northeast Ohio native Paul Newman, and Best Adapted Screenplay for *All the President's Men*. Goldman is responsible for the famous line "follow the money" in the latter-mentioned screenplay.

"Northeast Ohio is as viable as any other region in the country, despite its smaller size. Cleveland, in particular, has this low self-esteem thing working against it, and for some reason, the [residents] here can't seem to get beyond that. Maybe it's because the rest of the country is culpable to some degree, because no one outside of here can let the burning river thing go. Clevelanders definitely have a chip on their shoulder and that often manifests itself in creative ways."

— *Derek Hess, Artist and Co-Author,*
Please God Save Us

Langston Hughes:

Born in Joplin, Missouri, James Langston Hughes, the legendary African-American poet, playwright, and scribe, started writing in high school. As a teenager, Hughes moved with his mother to Cleveland. He eventually became a prolific writer. The Karamu House alum's most famous poem is "The Negro Speaks of Rivers," but in the more than 40 years between his first book and his death in 1967, he wrote 16 books of poems, a pair of novels, and a number of short stories, plays, operas, musicals, and children's poetry. His use of realism influenced an entire generation of American writers, including one of Hughes's biggest critics, James Baldwin.

Chuck Klosterman:

The North Dakota native came into his own in Akron as arts reporter at the Akron *Beacon Journal* before leaving for New York City and writing for a variety of entertainment publications including *Spin* magazine. Klosterman's timeline piece on what might have happened had Nirvana's Kurt Cobain not died created quite a stir, as did his collection of pop culture essays, *Sex, Drugs, and Cocoa Puffs: A Low Culture Manifesto*. In addition to his rock writing/reporting, Klosterman has also tackled sports writing for ESPN's Super Bowl and NCAA Final Four tournament coverage. Klosterman has also served as the Picador Guest Professor for Literature at the Institute for American Studies, University of Leipzig, Germany.

d.a. levy:

The Cleveland-based beat poet is considered by many as one of the godfathers of alternative media. Born Darryl Allan Levy, his hand-made, revolutionary approach to printing and circulating contemporary writings was the precursor to the "zine," or "fanzine," and hugely influential on the contemporary literature of today. His works often focused on sex, drugs, and politics. He and others used self-publishing to express concepts not found in the mainstream media. Through his Renegade Press and Seven Flowers Press, his "mimeograph revolution" landed him in trouble with the law for distributing obscene poetry to minors. When his self-press materials were confiscated, a May 1967 benefit event for him took place at the Case Institute of Technology featuring legendary poet Allen Ginsberg and others.

Sharing in a publishing revolution: local poet levy printed and circulated his (and other) contemporary writings in a precursor to the "zine." *(Cleveland* Press *Collection of the Cleveland State University Libraries)*

Steven Kotler:

The controversial writer/author attended school in Orange and immersed himself in the counterculture of Coventry in Cleveland Heights. His formative years in the latter helped him arrive at the idea that organized religion might well be the "the opiate of the masses," as Karl Marx once wrote. Along with Richard Dawkins's *The God Delusion*, Sam Harris's *The End of Faith: Religion, Terror, and the Future of Reason*, Kotler's *West of Jesus: Surfing, Science, and the Origins of Belief* was considered by critics as a signpost for disillusion in a post-September 11 U.S. Kotler studied under postmodern fiction author John Barth and has written for *Wired* and *Discover* magazines.

Toni Morrison:

The Lorain native and Nobel Prize-winning author Toni Morrison (born Chloe Anthony Wofford) is also an editor and professor. Her contemporary, postmodern novels are epic and extraordinarily full of depth and character. Her best-known works include *The Bluest Eye, Song of Solomon,* and *Beloved* – which won the Pulitzer Prize for Fiction in 1988. A decade later, *Beloved* was brought to the big screen in a film starring Oprah Winfrey. A survey of writers and literary critics conducted by *The New York Times* found *Beloved* the best work of American fiction of the past 25 years. In 2002, scholar Molefi Kete Asante named her to his list of "100 Greatest African Americans."

Lorain native Toni Morrison is the first African American to win the Nobel Prize for Literature. *(Cleveland* Press *Collection of the Cleveland State University Libraries)*

Jane Pratt:

The Oberlin College communications grad is the creator of *Sassy* and *Jane* magazines; both publications are credited with being seminal lifestyle publications for teenage girls and women, respectively. Both helped define what is now called "alternative media" and helped skew mass media reporting in a more hip and edgy way toward female audiences. Pratt's involvement in creating *Sassy* and *Jane* led to stints in several television projects for the Fox, VH-1, and Lifetime television networks. She has authored two books, *For Real: The Uncensored Truth About America's Teenagers* and *Beyond Beauty: Girls Speak Out on Looks, Style and Stereotypes.* She can currently be heard on Sirius/XM satellite radio's *Jane Radio* program.

Les Roberts:

After spending 24 years in Hollywood and writing for television shows including *The Lucy Show, The Andy Griffith Show, The Jackie Gleason Show*, and *The Man from U.N.C.L.E.*, Roberts won a private-eye novel contest and a new career trajectory was unveiled to him. Roberts is best known for his Cleveland-based private eye Milan

"I moved to Cleveland when I was 5. I went to Orange High School. And the one thing I can tell you is that the suburbs are the suburbs. Most of it was not particularly my interest at all. [But] I loved growing up around Coventry, though. Before subculture became normal culture, Cleveland was a great Midwestern city with that East Coast bluster and intelligence . . . In the late 70s and early 80s, if you were a weirdo in Cleveland, you were in the single greatest melting pot of counterculture I've ever seen. That whole scene was an incredible education, if you were open to everything."

— Steven Kotler, author, West of Jesus

Jacovich, whose adventures run over the course of more than 20 years, and 14 different novels. Jacovich is a rugged, blue-collar, working class divorcee with kids; Roberts's character has endeared him to Cleveland, a place Roberts calls home. Roberts has also been a jazz musician, professional actor, teacher, and businessman.

Connie Schultz:

Based in Avon, this Ashtabula-bred columnist writes for The *Plain Dealer* and is syndicated elsewhere. A contributor to the Huffington Post political blog, Schultz won the Pulitzer Prize for commentary in 2005. The Kent State University grad has written a pair of books: *Life Happens: And Other Unavoidable Truths*, and most recently *...and His Lovely Wife: A Memoir from the Woman Beside the Man.* The latter-mentioned book details her life on the campaign trail with husband U.S. Senator Sherrod Brown.

David Sedaris:

The Kent State University graduate humorist, comedian, and satirist has become one of the most successful and influential writers of his generation. He started in the early 90s when his *SantaLand Diaries* essay was broadcast on National Public Radio. He became a correspondent for NPR host Ira Glass's *This American Life* radio program. Shortly after his NPR stint, Sedaris published his first collection of essays and short stories, *Barrel Fever.* He has since penned five other collections of essays including *Naked, Dress Your Family in Corduroy and Denim*, and his most recent release, *When You Are Engulfed in Flames.* All are *New York Times* Best Sellers.

Dr. Benjamin Spock:

A one-time resident of Cleveland Heights, Spock is best known for authoring the 1946 book *The Common Sense Book of Baby and Child Care*, a "how-to" guide on parenting that helped parents rear generations of kids all over the globe. Spock was a child development professional at what is now known as Case Western Reserve University.

Thornton Wilder:

The author and playwright was an Oberlin College student before moving on to Yale. He won the Pulitzer Prize three different times — once for the novel *The Bridge of San*

Luis Rey in 1928 and twice for the plays *Our Town* (1938) and *The Skin of Our Teeth* (1942). *Our Town*'s characters and fictional setting of Grover's Corners continue to endure as a snapshot of American life. The play is revived regularly in theaters across the country.

Mark Winegardner:

"A great American novel about ... Cleveland? Yes, children, this is the real deal." So proclaimed horror novelist extraordinaire Stephen King in a column in *Entertainment Weekly* in 2006. He was speaking of Winegardner's *Crooked River Burning*, a love letter to Winegardner's hometown. Born in Bryan, Ohio, the author wrote for the Cleveland *Free Times* before moving on to national venues like *GQ*, *Playboy*, *The Sporting News*, and *The New York Times Magazine*. Winegardner is best known for a pair of novels – *The Godfather Returns* and *The Godfather's Revenge* – which revived Mario Puzo's legendary mafia family, the Corleones. There's little doubt that both novels will become films or a television miniseries at some point. Winegardner is currently the Burroway Professor of English and Director of the Creative Writing Program at Florida State University in Tallahassee.

Roger Zelazny:

Born in Euclid, Zelazny's science fiction and fantasy novels and short stories earned him three Nebula awards and six Hugo awards — including one for the novel . . . *And Call Me Conrad*, which tied for the award with Frank Herbert's celebrated novel *Dune* in 1966. Zelazny worked for the Social Security Administration office in Cleveland by day and wrote at night. When he died of cancer in 1995 at age 58, Zelazny was one of the most beloved and celebrated sci-fi fiction writers in the world. During the 90s, two unfinished novels (*Lord Demon* and *Donnerjack*) were completed by writer Jane Lindskold. A recently discovered Zelazny manuscript, a hardboiled noir mystery *The Dead Man's Brother*, was released in 2009.

Did You Know? **Children's author David "Dav" Pilkey, who penned and drew the *Captain Underpants* book series, was born in Cleveland.**

Lorain native Helen Steiner Rice was acclaimed during her career as "America's beloved inspirational poet laureate" for her religious and uplifting poetry; her work was featured on the Lawrence Welk show in the 50s, which launched collections of her written works into multiple printings.

In the early 20th century Cleveland-bred writer and political activist Charles W. Chestnut wrote novels about African-American life. Chestnut is one of the first mixed-race authors to tackle race in print and was quite popular during his heyday.

Best-selling novelist Tracy Chevalier, known for her work *Girl With the Pearl Earring,* is an Oberlin College graduate. *Earring* was recently adapted for a film starring actress Scarlett Johansson.

Music

From Cleveland expatriate and singer-songwriter Tracy Chapman to Nine Inch Nails helmsman and creative catalyst Trent Reznor, to a diverse range of artists including Bone Thugs -N- Harmony, Joe Walsh, Henry Mancini, Pere Ubu, Devo, and Frankie Yankovic, Northeast Ohio's sheer variety of music is stunning. While a wide range of hip-hop, alternative, and metal music appears to be "what's next" for the region, it has continually (and consistently) produced a wide range of great rock and roll and singer-songwriters.

Alternative Press Magazine:

Starting out as a photocopied "fanzine" over 20 years ago by founder Mike Shea, *Alternative Press* (AP) was launched in Cleveland and has remained here for the duration of its publication. Its editorial focus on cutting-edge alternative rock and roll music has made it widely influential. AP has featured bands long before they've broken into the mainstream; the editorial staff's authority can now be heard on Sirius/XM Satellite Radio. It is a major sponsor of the Van's Warped Tour alternative music festival that tours the country annually.

The Black Keys:

This independent-minded, blues-rock duo from Akron has accomplished a great deal in their short, eight-year career. With a musical approach that recalls everything from Screamin' Jay Hawkins to Robert Johnson, Dan Auerbach (guitars/vocals) and Patrick Carney (drums/production) tend to focus on the grit and melody in their "lo-fi" and minimally altered songs. They recently joined fellow Akronites Devo and Chrissie Hynde of the Pretenders on stage at the Akron Civic Theater for a benefit concert for Barack Obama.

Meet the New Boss, Same as the Old Boss? Akron indie rockers The Black Keys and Devo share a moment during a Barack Obama presidential fundraiser at the Akron Civic in 2008. *(Photo by Janet Macoska)*

Bone Thugs -N- Harmony:

Formed by members Krayzie Bone, Bizzy Bone, Layzie Bone, and Wish Bone, the acclaimed hip-hop outfit from Cleveland's Glenville neighborhood made a big splash in the 90s, teaming up with producer DJ U-Neek for the majority of their recordings. The group won a Grammy Award for Best Rap Performance with their song "Tha Crossroads" from their *E 1999 Eternal* album in 1997. The group lays claim to being the only group to collaborate with rappers Tupac "2Pac" Shakur, Chris "The Notoroius B.I.G." Wallace, Chris "Big Punisher" Rios, and Eazy-E (from N.W.A.).

Jim Brickman:

The adult contemporary pianist and songwriter grew up in Cleveland and attended both Cleveland Institute of Music and Case Western Reserve University. Brickman's lighter, "lifestyle-music" has yielded over a dozen CD releases, a trio of *Billboard* chart-topping hits, gold and platinum records, and a Grammy Award nomination. A frequent collaborator with friend and fellow Clevelander vocalist Anne Cochran, Brickman has played at the Ford Theater, Carnegie Hall, and the White House and has been featured in several PBS television specials. Brickman hosts his own syndicated radio show, *Your Weekend with Jim Brickman.*

Pianist Jim Brickman has released over a dozen successful records. *(Photo by Janet Macoska)*

The Cars:

The chart-topping pop band from Boston came together when bandleaders Ric Ocasek (singer/guitars) and Clevelander Benjamin Orr (bass/vocals) met at a party in Columbus, Ohio. After rounding out the band's lineup with keyboardist Greg

Benjamin Orr, bassist for The Cars, was responsible for the band's most memorable ballad, "Drive." *(Photo by Janet Macoska)*

Hawkes, guitarist Elliot Easton, and drummer David Robinson, the group made a full-court press in the Boston scene and ended up breaking nationwide on FM radio. Their career spanned from the late 70s through 1984's chart-topping album *Heartbeat City*. The band's biggest hits include "Just What I Needed," "My Best Friend's Girl," "Let's Go," "Magic," "Hello Again," and the Orr-led "Drive," which became the band's biggest hit. At one point, both Ocasek and Orr lived in Shaker Heights.

Tracy Chapman:

Born in Cleveland in the mid-60s, singer-songwriter Chapman began appearing in coffeehouses while attending Tufts University in Massachusetts. After graduation, she signed with SBK Records and released her debut album *Tracy Chapman* – a critically hailed, *Billboard* chart-topping effort that spawned two gigantic hits ("Fast Car," "Talkin' Bout a Revolution") and sold millions of copies. The album also earned Chapman four Grammy Awards. Some credit Chapman for single-handedly launching the female singer-songwriter movement that became so popular in the 90s, and which culminated in

Cleveland native and Grammy Award-winner Tracy Chapman. *(Peter Chakerian collection)*

the Sarah McLachlan-founded Lilith Fair tour. Chapman has released seven other albums, including the 2008 effort *Our Bright Future*.

Chimaira:

The ten-year-old, Cleveland-based heavy/power-metal band is part of that musical genre's resurgence. The group, led by the sharp, angular, and downtuned guitar riffs of Rob Arnold, has had a string of successful albums and tours, including dates with fellow Cleveland metal act Mushroomhead under the moniker "The Kings of Cleveland." Chimaira's last CD (2009's *The Infection*) debuted at number 30 in the *Billboard* Top 200 Chart.

Cleveland Agora Theatre and Ballroom:

The seminal Cleveland rock and roll club may have been located in three different spots in the city — settling in the old WHK building in 1984, where it exists today — but it has been the spotlight in identifying and bringing rock bands and artists to prominence. Acts like Todd Rundgren, Grand Funk Railroad, ZZ Top, Bruce Springsteen, The Raspberries, and others went on to larger audiences after delivering groundbreaking gigs at the Agora. At one point, there were 13 different Agora locations; Cleveland's location is the only one to remain.

Cleveland International Records:

The independent record label was launched in Cleveland in 1977 by founder/recording luminary Steve Popovich. One of the first releases that Popovich's label offered to the public for purchase was Meat Loaf's album *Bat Out of Hell*, a collaboration between Loaf (a singer and *Rocky Horror Picture Show* actor born Marvin Lee Aday)

Todd Rundgren was one of the Cleveland Agora's regular performers and earned for it a diehard following in Cleveland. *(Photo by Janet Macoska)*

Ian Hunter (right) with his Cleveland International Records alums backstage at the Cleveland Agora. Hunter is responsible for the classic rock anthems "All The Young Dudes" (with Mott the Hoople) and "Cleveland Rocks." *(Photo by Janet Macoska)*

"The popular culture that has emerged from [Northeast Ohio] is the story of what happens when nobody is paying attention. In Northeast Ohio . . . the idea of a 'garage band' is literal. In New York City, and on the Sunset Strip [of West Hollywood, California], nobody has a garage. Those people have to grow up on stage, and by default, they are artificial; they are literally born of artifice. Here . . . everybody has a garage. And a full-size bedroom. And a basement. And, often, a barn. There are all sorts of spaces for self-discovery and also spaces simply to hide. Extend this to the abandoned industrial landscape, and you have an entire playground of creative discovery and also a warren of places to stop and think about what's happening to you and around you. The art is bound to be specific, real, slow-cooked, and hard-won."

— David Giffels, Author, All the Way Home

and songwriter Jim Steinman. The album has sold over 40 million copies to date. Cleveland International Records went on to release music by Southside Johnny, Ronnie Spector, The Rovers, David Allen Coe, B.J. Thomas, and Ian Hunter, best known for the Northeast Ohio anthem "Cleveland Rocks." The label has also been responsible for making a wide range of polka releases available to the public, including those of Cleveland "polka king" Frankie Yankovic.

Cobra Verde:

The neo-glam rock outfit fronted by Cleveland *Plain Dealer* nightlife writer John Petkovic formed from the ashes of influential Ohio bands Death of Samantha and Gem. The band has the distinction for being Robert Pollard's "backing band" for his ever-changing garage rock outfit Guided by Voices. It has appeared on the television series *The OC* as a Foreigner tribute band. The band's last two efforts, 2005's *Copycat Killers* and 2008's *Haven't Slept All Year*, are their most critically acclaimed.

Marc Cohn:

The Cleveland-born singer-songwriter, Beachwood High School and Oberlin College graduate, is best known for his song "Walking in Memphis," which earned him the Grammy Award for Best New Artist in 1991. Cohn has released four studio albums to date and is married to ABC News journalist Elizabeth Vargas. Cohn survived being shot in the head during an attempted carjacking. His most recent album, *Join the Parade*, delves into this life-altering event.

Beachwood High School alum Marc Cohn's award-winning 1991 single "Walking in Memphis" is still wildly popular nearly 20 years since it first aired. *(Photo courtesy of MarcCohn.net)*

David Allen Coe:

The country singer-songwriter from Akron is best known for penning the hit single "Take This Job and Shove It," a song which became a hit for singer Johnny Paycheck. In and out of trouble for much of his early life, Coe is as controversial on record as he has been in life. Coe and his "outlaw country" music continues the tradition developed by "The Man in Black" Johnny Cash.

Devo:

The New Wave band formed in Akron in 1973 and has proven influential during the last 35 years. Pioneers of MTV and the music video revolution of the 80s, the band is best remembered for their hit single "Whip It." The group's synth-pop quirkiness, however, decorated with social commentary and sci-fi themes, was really intended as more of a lifestyle and art movement. The band's watershed effort, *Freedom of Choice*, sold over one million copies in the U.S. Devo's look was an unmistakable one; their yellow jumpsuits and red "energy dome" (also called flowerpot) helmets have become a calling card for the band.

Akron's New Wave icons Devo pose in front of the Chili Dog Mac in their hometown in 1978. *(Photo by Janet Macoska)*

Don Dixon:

A Canton native, Dixon is one of the pivotal record producers of the 80s, specializing in what critics have dubbed "jangle pop." A singer, songwriter, bassist, and self-professed "knob-twiddler," his credits include writing, producing, and performing with an encyclopedia of musicians including Mary Chapin Carpenter, Joe Cocker, Hootie and the Blowfish, R.E.M., The Smithereens, Ronnie Spector, Matthew Sweet, and his wife (and fellow Cantonite, singer-songwriter) Marti Jones. His longtime touring band, which includes Jamie Hoover and Jim Brock, recently re-named themselves Don Dixon & the Jump Rabbits and perform together regularly.

Danny Elfman:

The Oberlin College graduate and enigmatic Oingo Boingo frontman of 20 years is seldom referred to in relation to his rock and roll career because of his award-winning success as a film score composer. An Academy Award nominee and Grammy winner, Elfman's playful compositions are most often heard in friend/film director Tim Burton's works, including *Pee-Wee's Big Adventure, Batman, Edward Scissorhands,* and *Charlie and the Chocolate Factory.* Elfman is also revered for his sonic brushstrokes in the cult classic film *The Nightmare Before Christmas.* He has scored over two dozen films and has also provided the soundtrack to television shows *Tales From the Crypt, The Simpsons,* and *Desperate Housewives.*

Filter:

Formed by one-time member of Nine Inch Nails and former Rocky River resident Richard Patrick, this industrial rock band took a pop approach. Patrick formed the band with fellow resident Brian Liesegang (no longer with the band) and recorded their debut *Short Bus*, which featured the single "Hey Man, Nice Shot." The group's shifting lineup has had Patrick as a constant over the years; the group's biggest hit, a non-industrial pop ballad called "Take a Picture," carries on in the soundtracks to several motion pictures.

Alan Freed:

Born Albert James Freed, and known to his fans as "Moondog" and the "Father of Rock and Roll," he was a revolutionary disc jockey who lived in Shaker Heights for a time. He coined the term "rock and roll" (which he attributed to African-American rhythm and blues music) and honed his broadcasting skills at radio stations in Akron and Cleveland before gaining an opportunity to play and promote this variety of music in New York. Shamed by a scandal involving "payola" (slang term for accepting money from recording companies and others for preferential radio play) Freed left the industry heartbroken. His influence, however, carries on today. Most popular music from the last 50 years and the Rock and Roll Hall of Fame and Museum itself are just the beginning of Freed's legacy.

The father of Rock and Roll, Cleveland disc jockey Alan Freed not only coined the term for popular music, but had a hand in organizing the first real rock concert — The Moondog Coronation Ball. Need any more be said? *(Cleveland* Press *Collection of the Cleveland State University Libraries)*

Macy Gray:

The neo-soul vocalist and Canton native born Natalie Renee McIntyre has a sandpaper vocal style that recalls Billie Holiday and Kim Carnes. Her Grammy award-winning song "I Try" (from her 1999 debut album *On How Life Is*) is still her most popular work. Gray's popularity in the United Kingdom far exceeds her popularity in the U.S. today (at least as of press time), but the star has been attempting a comeback and recording a new album under the pseudonym "Nemesis Jaxson."

Dave Grohl:

Born in Warren, the drummer for the seminal alternative rock band Nirvana has almost completely eclipsed his early days with that defining Seattle band with his own outfit, Foo Fighters. Grohl contributed on several of Nirvana's recordings, including their two biggest albums, the 1991 breakthrough album *Nevermind* and the 1993 follow-up *In Utero*. His drumming also propelled the band's extraordinary live effort, *Unplugged in New York*. Considered a workaholic by some of his peers, Grohl has pushed a shifting lineup of the Foos through a decade-plus long career, seven full-length albums, and a seemingly endless string of radio hits including "Big Me," "Everlong," "Times Like These," "Learn To Fly," and "My Hero."

Once the drummer for seminal alt-rockers Nirvana, Dave Grohl now fronts the band Foo Fighters. Grohl is pictured here in concert at Cleveland State University's Wolstein Center. *(Photo by William Rieter)*

Jalacy J. "Screamin' Jay" Hawkins:

The blues singer, pianist, and Cleveland native has been called "the original shock rocker" for ghoulish performances during his mid-50s heyday. His shows and legendary song "I Put a Spell on You" are said to have influenced a whole host of ghastly (at the time) rock and roll artists, from the manic band The Crazy World of Arthur Brown in the 60s, to 70s icons Alice Cooper and original goth rockers Black Sabbath.

"During the early days of Alan [Freed]'s career, there was a lot of back and forth in the car from Shaker Heights to the studio in Cleveland — him practicing his meter the whole way there. [Radio] was the most important thing to him to become a DJ. If there was anything about Cleveland that fostered his experience more than anything else, it was because [the city] was a blank canvas that allowed him the opportunity to do what he wanted to do and create and progress . . . and it still is that way, to a large degree. Cleveland was large enough to enjoy success, yet small enough to explore ideas and try your hand at anything. Cleveland was Alan's springboard; his career might not have happened if he hadn't found a place where everything wasn't already defined."

— Judith Fisher-Freed

Chrissie Hynde:

Perhaps Akron's favorite daughter and former Kent State University student, Hynde formed the punk rock band The Pretenders in London in 1978. The band has had several personnel changes throughout the years; Hynde and her toasty-tough vocals and rhythm guitar playing have been the only constant. Inducted into the Rock and Roll Hall of Fame in 2005, Hynde's band has produced a slew of songs over the years, including "Brass In Pocket," "Back on the Chain Gang," "Middle of the Road," "Don't Get Me Wrong," and the Northeast Ohio anthem on regional decline, "My City is Gone." A social justice advocate and animal rights activist, Hynde opened a vegetarian restaurant in Akron in 2007 called VegiTerranean.

Akron native Chrissie Hynde kicked down doors for all female rockers with her band The Pretenders' self-titled debut in 1980. *(Photo by Janet Macoska)*

Marti Jones:

The singer-songwriter (and wife to jangle rock producer Don Dixon) was born in Uniontown and recorded her first album as a member of the band Color Me Gone in the early 80s. Her first solo album, *Unsophisticated Time* was produced by Dixon. They were married shortly after, and Dixon has continued to produce her albums. Jones has worked with a number of acclaimed musicians including Marshall Crenshaw, Mitch Easter (who, with Dixon, produced the legendary band R.E.M.), Paul Carrack, and T-Bone Burnett.

Sammy Kaye:

Born in Lakewood, Sammy "Kaye" Zarnocay, Jr. was a revered Big Band jazz bandleader whose records helped a generation through World War II. A Rocky River High School graduate, his records and radio performances were as legendary as his "Swing and Sway with Sammy Kaye" tagline. Kaye's band charted over 100 hit singles. Kaye is a Big Band and Jazz Hall of

Sammy Kaye's prolific body of work includes over 100 hit records. He helped the U.S. get through World War II from right here in Cleveland. *(Cleveland Press Collection of the Cleveland State University Libraries)*

Fame inductee. He also earned a star on the Hollywood Walk of Fame for his musical contributions to U.S. culture.

Maynard James Keenan:

The Ravenna native is best known as the front man, vocalist, and lyricist for the Grammy award-winning neo-progressive rock act Tool and the alternative rock supergroup A Perfect Circle. The former band's critical highpoint, 2001's semi-concept album *Lateralus*, debuted on the *Billboard* album chart at #1 and pushed the band into playing arenas worldwide. A winemaker and stand-up comedian in his spare time, Keenan has also released some campier solo music works under the monikers Puscifer and Green Jello.

Levert:

More than just a dance band, the family name Levert is synonymous with great grooves. The surnamed group launched in Cleveland in the mid-80s by Sean and Gerald Levert — sons of the legendary O'Jays founder Eddie Levert — had a strong hit single with the song "Casanova," part of a 12-year run of rhythm and blues hits.

Tommy LiPuma:

The chairman of the Verve Music Group was born in Cleveland and has worked

Chairman of the Verve Music Group LiPuma (right) embraces jazz legend and fellow Clevelander Jimmy Scott. *(Photo by Janet Macoska)*

with a plethora of musical heavyweights including Al Jarreau, George Benson, Natalie Cole, the jazz-fusion outfit Yellowjackets, fellow Clevelander Jimmy Scott, and the legendary Miles Davis. He produced the posthumous, father-daughter duet "Unforgettable" between Cole and her father Nat "King" Cole, which earned him one of his Grammy Awards. He cut his first record with Canton act and 2005 Rock and Roll Hall of Fame inductees The O'Jays. LiPuma has also been instrumental in the career of jazz piano chanteuse Diana Krall.

Robert Lockwood, Jr.:

The Grammy award-winning bluesman was (and is) a Cleveland institution. Born in Arkansas, Lockwood arrived in Cleveland in the early 60s and maintained residence here while playing and recording some of his best work. The emotive guitar player's weekly performances at Fat Fish Blue in downtown Cleveland carried on well past Lockwood's 90th birthday.

Channeling the blues: Robert Lockwood, Jr. was a mainstay at the corner of Prospect Avenue and Ontario Street. *(Photo by Walter Novak)*

A Little Italy native, Henry Mancini is best known for his jazzy theme to *The Pink Panther* series of films and for the theme to *Moon River*. *(Cleveland Press Collection of the Cleveland State University Libraries)*

Henry Mancini:

Born in Cleveland's Little Italy neighborhood, the Academy Award-winning American composer, conductor, and arranger is best known for his jazzy theme to *The Pink Panther* series of films and for the theme to *Moon River*. Mancini is responsible for dozens of soundtracks to television and film, including *Music from Peter Gunn, Breakfast at Tiffany's, The Great Race*, and *Victor/Victoria*. He won several Grammy Awards including a "Lifetime Achievement Award" in 1995.

Marilyn Manson:

Tall, lanky Cantonite and vocalist Marilyn Manson (nee Brian Hugh Warner) took a page out of the Iggy Pop and Alice Cooper playbooks when he launched his shock rock music career in the 90s. Influenced by a religious upbringing and with a penchant for glam rock and a taste for the bizarre, Manson formed a band called the Spooky Kids, and the members took their stage names from Hollywood stars and serial killers. Manson crossed paths with Trent Reznor (of Nine Inch Nails) who recognized the singer's talent and signed him to his Nothing Records label. Manson went on to release a string of hit albums including the watershed *Antichrist Superstar* (a play on the Andrew Lloyd Webber/Tim Rice rock opera) album.

Controversial Cantonite Marilyn Manson (nee Brian Warner) made huge waves with his 1996 shock-rock masterpiece *Antichrist Superstar. (Photo by Walter Novak)*

Leo Mintz:

Without Mintz, some say there's no Alan Freed and maybe no "Rock and Roll" term, either. Mintz was the father of the modern record store (Record Rendezvous) and was a "big idea man" for legendary DJ Alan Freed, as detailed in *Big Beat Heat: Alan Freed and the Early Years of Rock & Roll.* Mintz founded Record Rendezvous in 1938 on Prospect Avenue downtown; he reportedly was the first record store purveyor to display records in bins for browsing in lieu of keeping them behind the counter as was customary for the time. Mintz also offered his customers listening booths and in-store appearances by recording artists. This pioneering approach to record sales, in conjunction with Mintz's tutelage of Freed, helped define a generation and helped make Cleveland the "Home of Rock and Roll." Mintz's grandson Douglas Trattner writes in his *Moon Guide to Cleveland* that the term "Rock and Roll" was suggested to Freed by Mintz.

Masked marauders of metal music, Cleveland thrash-metal band Mushroomhead has won a devoted legion of fans with an aggressive sound and nightmarish appearance. *(Peter Chakerian collection)*

Mushroomhead:

Bringing together alternative metal music, electro-industrial sounds and bleak, gothic costuming, this Cleveland band formed in 1993 and has enjoyed national success with their records, even as they maintain their cult status at home. The group's music has made it to feature films (most notably *Freddy vs. Jason*) and the band's distinctive "X-face" masks have struck comparisons to fellow costumed rockers GWAR and Slipknot. Mushroomhead most recently toured with heavy metal legends Slayer and Canton's own Marilyn Manson in the 2009 summer Mayhem Festival.

"Trent Reznor has been brilliant in everything he's done. Even though he's not living here anymore, and none of us really know what he thinks about Cleveland these days, you can hear his experience here every time you play his music. That edge, the grit, the dark and brooding, but also the inventiveness and structure and ownership he's made with both industrial and electronic music. You can take Trent out of Cleveland, but you can't take Cleveland out of Trent. That's just the way it is. That attitude, that sound, aggression. Especially from [the Nine Inch Nails] album The Fragile *on, he's been absolutely dead-on."*

— Derek Hess, Artist and Co-Author, Please God Save Us

Trent Reznor (a.k.a. Nine Inch Nails, NIN):

Alum of famed Cleveland bands including Lucky Pierre and Exotic Birds, Reznor formed the industrial rock act in 1988. Though it started out as a solo project, Reznor gathered a rotating group of musicians to reproduce the sounds he created on his 1989 debut, *Pretty Hate Machine*. Reznor is the main producer and singer-songwriter for NIN and has been solely responsible for its artistic direction. Since his debut, Reznor has sold millions of copies of his albums *Broken, The Downward Spiral, The Fragile*, and *With Teeth*. His success is multi-faceted: he is credited with popularizing industrial music by personalizing its mechanical sound (some say Reznor put the "I" in industrial music). He has also been an early adopter of technological advances in music production and sales. Reznor and his latest lineup of the band just wrapped up a tour with alternative rockers Jane's Addiction (with whom NIN launched the successful Lollapalooza Festival in 1991).

Trent Reznor seemed to single-handedly personalize the "industrial rock" genre. He also single-handedly crafted his debut album *Pretty Hate Machine*. *(Photo by Walter Novak)*

The O'Jays:

Best known for singles "Love Train" and "For the Love of Money," this Canton rhythm and blues act was originally called the Triumphs. Formed in the late 50s by high school pals Eddie Levert, Walter Williams, Bill Isles, Bobby Massey, and William Powell, the group was inducted into the Rock and Roll Hall of Fame in 2005.

Pere Ubu:

If there's such a thing as a soundtrack for the industrial downturn of Northeast Ohio and the stress and anxiety of its residents, then 70s iconoclastic Pere Ubu has most certainly tapped it. Led by the presence of singer David Thomas (a.k.a. "Crocus Behemoth"), the Cleveland band's shifting lineup has led to a body of work that is equal parts art-punk, post-punk, and performance art. The band has carried on for decades. It has delivered sounds and soundscapes tantamount to literary post-modern fiction or like a Jim Jarmusch film for the ears. The band continues to record and perform a handful of shows every year. Their most recently recorded work, *Why I Hate Women*, was critically hailed as among the band's best efforts.

The Raspberries (featuring Eric Carmen):

Launched in the 60s in Lyndhurst, this power-pop garage band with a British Invasion sound was led by singer-songwriter Carmen. Carmen, a Cleveland Institute of Music student, was joined by friends Wally Bryson, Dave Smalley, and Jim Bonfanti from the local Cleveland band

One of Cleveland's most influential underground bands, Pere Ubu was caught backstage at the Cleveland Agora in April 1978. *(Photo by Janet Macoska)*

Eric Carmen strums on stage during The Raspberries' reunion/homecoming show at the House of Blues in Cleveland in 2004. *(Photo by Janet Macoska)*

The Choir. The group peaked with the single "Go All The Way" before breaking up in 1975. Carmen went on to write the hit single "Almost Paradise" (from the film *Footloose*) and record the hit singles "All By Myself" and "Hungry Eyes," the latter from the hit motion picture, *Dirty Dancing*. Carmen still lives in Cleveland and recently reformed the Raspberries for a reunion tour.

Robert Quine:

While this Akron-based guitarist never reached a level of success befitting his talents, Quine was hugely influential on a number artists including Richard Hell & the Voidoids, Brian Eno, Lou Reed, John Zorn, Matthew Sweet, and Tom Waits. He is a relative of Dan Auerbach of the Akron blues-rock duo The Black Keys.

Rock and Roll legends (from left to right) Billy Joel, Chuck Berry, and Pete Townshend of The Who partake in the groundbreaking ceremony for Cleveland's main pop culture temple, the Rock and Roll Hall of Fame and Museum. *(Photo by Janet Macoska)*

Rock and Roll Hall of Fame and Museum:

The museum, which opened in Cleveland in 1995, celebrates the rich history and legacy of rock and roll music. The Rock Hall groundbreaking and grand opening brought in rock music luminaries from all over the world. A concert of more than five hours at Cleveland Municipal Stadium helped open the Rock Hall to the world and featured some of the final live performances given by inductees The Kinks and Johnny Cash. The Rock and Roll Hall of Fame Foundation, which helps oversee and aids in the direction of the museum, has come under fire for a number of reasons, including the choices of inductees and holding the ceremonies in New York City. Recently, the Foundation announced that inductions will be held in Cleveland every three years beginning in 2009. The Rock Hall celebrated the opening of an Annex in New York City in 2008 and cooperated in building a music archive on the Cuyahoga Community College Metro campus.

Swingos:

The renowned Cleveland landmark opened in the 60s as a restaurant and "celebrity inn" that hosted a slew of musical stars including Elvis Presley, Frank Sinatra, The Doors, Pink Floyd, and Kiss. As legend has it, if you had a key to a room at Swingos when rock and roll royalty was in town, you were in for quite a party. Swingos was fictionally immortalized in the 2000 motion picture *Almost Famous.*

Decades ago, keys like this one meant an unforgettable rock and roll party. *(Photo by Peter Chakerian)*

Telarc "Digital" International Corporation:

The independent classical and jazz record label was founded in 1977 by classically trained musicians and teachers Jack Renner and Robert Woods. Telarc was one of the first labels to begin recording music using the pioneering technique of 20-bit analog-to-digital conversion. Telarc (now part of Concord Music Group) has released works by marquee musical acts The Cleveland Orchestra, including The London Symphony Orchestra, Dave Brubeck, Manhattan Transfer, and Arturo Sandoval.

WMMS 100.7 FM:

The legendary Cleveland radio station might be a shell of its former self these days, but during the 70s and 80s, the FM station was nationally revered and is credited with introducing a host of now-legendary rock acts, including David Bowie, Bruce Springsteen, Rush, Roxy Music, and others to national audiences. WMMS virtually redefined what a rock and roll radio station should sound like. For a long time, stations across the country tried to emulate

"The biggest thing is that being here [in Cleveland] gives you a sense of grounding . . . we weren't frequently visited by [record] label employees and managers playing us with expensive lunches, dinners, and a good table at a strip club, unlike people who work in commercial radio, most of whom need to be taken down to Public Square and given the Mussolini head-kick treatment. We've sorted through hype fairly well and didn't rely on some metropolitan hipster from New York or Los Angeles telling us . . . 'Fantastic! You need to get on this.'"

— Jason Pettigrew, Editor-in-Chief, Alternative Press *magazine*

"Chrissie Hynde was the first female to be the iconic figurehead of a true, great, authentic, non-novelty rock band. The first. In those first couple years, Chrissie Hynde was Robert Plant; she was Buddy Holly; she was Bob Marley; she was Martha Reeves. And not only because she was a profoundly good singer and songwriter, but also because she had a profoundly good band behind her. In every aspect, the Pretenders' debut album, and everything I've seen and heard of their live shows in the original incarnation, answers any question about their legitimacy as one of the great rock and roll machines of our lifetime . . . In fact, I think Chrissie Hynde proves my theory of any great rock band whose singer plays guitar — she/he is almost always most probably virtually unable to play guitar — and the band is better because of it. That's where greatness begins."

— David Giffels, Author, We Are Devo!

the Cleveland-based station. WMMS was critical in organizing the campaign that ultimately led to Cleveland winning the Rock and Roll Hall of Fame and Museum.

The James Gang (with Joe Walsh, front right) reunited briefly in 1996 to perform for voters at a presidential rally at Cleveland State University, one aimed at helping the re-election of President Bill Clinton. *(Photo by William Rieter)*

Joe Walsh:

The catalyst of The James Gang and wiseacre "guitarslinger" in the legendary country rock band The Eagles, Walsh is most certainly one of the region's favorite adopted sons. He formed The James Gang in 1966 with Jim Fox (drums), Tom Kriss (bass), Phil Giallombardo (keyboards), Ronnie Silverman and Glen Schwartz (guitars). The band's *The James Gang Rides Again* album is considered a classic album. Walsh replaced Bernie Leadon in The Eagles and was a part of the band's biggest commercial success, the album *Hotel California*. Walsh has had some modest success as a solo act, but a reunion of both of his best-known bands has recently kept him busy. Walsh was inducted with The Eagles into the Rock and Roll Hall of Fame in 1998.

Scott Weiland:

The Chagrin Falls native, born Scott Richard Kline, is best known as the lead singer for the 90s alternative rock band Stone Temple Pilots, a quartet that scored a number of hits during that decade including "Interstate Love Song," "Wicked Garden," "Plush,"

Scott Weiland (with the supershort blonde hair) poses with his band Stone Temple Pilots for a promotional photo session to support their debut album, *Core*. *(Peter Chakerian collection)*

"Big Empty," and "Vasoline." The group disbanded after Weiland left. In between solo albums he served as the front man for the band Velvet Revolver with former members of the metal band Guns N' Roses. He joined the reunited Stone Temple Pilots for a reunion tour in 2008. Many of Weiland's contemporaries have proclaimed him one of the most influential vocalists from that decade.

Bobby Womack:

The Cleveland native and Rock and Roll Hall of Fame inductee (2009) is best known for his pioneering rhythm and blues sound. A side man for a number of acts including Sam Cooke and the Rolling Stones, Womack's solo career stretched across three decades and yielded the hits "Woman's Gotta Have It" and "That's the Way I Feel About Cha."

Frankie Yankovic:

Known as "America's Polka King," the Slovenian band leader and squeeze box master has been one of Cleveland's favorite sons. Raised in Cleveland's Collinwood neighborhood, Yankovic was a young apprentice to the accordion. By the late 40s he had secured his first recorded hit "Just Because." Yankovic appears on over 200 recorded albums of music and performed with a who's who in entertainment over the years — from Chet Atkins and The Everly Brothers, to Doris Day and Drew Carey. He won the first ever Best Polka Recording Grammy Award in 1986.

Popular Music with a Nod and a Wink to Northeast Ohio

Singer Scott Weiland of Stone Temple Pilots recently released a solo album called *Happy in Galoshes.* Its first single is titled "Missing Cleveland." *(Photo by William Rieter)*

Guitarist Pete Townsend of The Who wrote the song "Sheraton Gibson" during a tour where Cleveland and a subsequently depressing tour stop thereafter caused him to sing longingly for the city. *(Photo by Janet Macoska)*

"Akron City Love" (Ace Boogie)

"Burn On" (Randy Newman)

"Chagrin Falls" (Tragically Hip)

"Christmas in Cleveland" (The Raveonettes)

"Cleveland" (All Time Quarterback)

"Cleveland" (Jewel)

"Cleveland is the City" (Bone Thugs-N-Harmony)

"The Cleveland Polka" (Frankie Yankovic)

"Cleveland Rocks" (Ian Hunter, The Presidents of the United States of America)

"Cuyahoga" (R.E.M.)

"Drunk on the Moon" (Tom Waits)

"Heart of Rock and Roll" (Huey Lewis & the News)

"Let's Move to Cleveland" (Frank Zappa)

"Look Out Cleveland" (The Band)

"Mean Night in Cleveland" (Cactus)

"Missing Cleveland" (Scott Weiland)

"My City Was Gone" (Pretenders)

"Ohio" (Crosby, Stills, Nash & Young)

"Pancho & Lefty" (Townes Van Zandt, Willie Nelson, Merle Haggard)

"Rednecks" (Randy Newman)

"Sheraton Gibson" (Pete Townshend)

"Wreck of the Edmund Fitzgerald" (Gordon Lightfoot)

"Youngstown" (Bruce Springsteen)

Did You Know?

Trent Reznor played a role in a fictional band in Paul Schrader's 1987 film *Light of Day*, set in Cleveland and starring Joan Jett and Michael J. Fox.

Multi-platinum award-winning producer Michael Seifert, a Cleveland native, has produced records for Tori Amos, Fountains of Wayne, Colbie Caillat, Guided By Voices, and several famous Northeast Ohio acts including Levert, Robert Lockwood, Jr., Nicholas Megalis, Kate Voegele, and Bone Thugs -N- Harmony.

Joan Jett (left) and actor Michael J. Fox trade guitar licks in this picture, reprising at a film release party their roles from the film *Light of Day*. *(Photo by Janet Macoska)*

One hit wonder Dee-Lite's singer/DJ Lady Miss Kier was born in Youngstown. Dee-Lite's "Groove is in the Heart" featured another Ohioan, Cincinnati's Bootsy Collins, on bass guitar.

Northeast Ohio has quite a few Rock and Roll Hall of Fame Hall inductees, including Chrissie Hynde, The O'Jays, Joe Walsh, Bobby Womack, and Alan Freed. Freed was part of the Rock Hall's first-ever class of inductees in 1986.

Alan Freed's ashes were interred inside the walls of the Rock and Roll Hall of Fame and Museum at the wishes of the iconic DJ's family's wishes.

Maynard James Keenan of Tool and Trent Reznor of Nine Inch Nails were briefly in an alternative rock act together called Tapeworm.

The 1991 debut album ***Gish*** by alternative rockers The Smashing Pumpkins was named for actress Lillian Gish.

Ken Forissi of the band Love was born in Cleveland. Long before it was fashionable, or even socially acceptable, his

Trent Reznor of Nine Inch Nails personalized industrial music, then went on to revolutionize the way people consume his music through technology, free internet album releases, and viral online marketing. *(Photo by William Rieter)*

psychedelic garage rock band sported a multi-racial lineup. The band was short-lived, but continues to be influential.

Often referred to as the "Kings of Cleveland" by their fans, the bands Chimaira and Mushroomhead are from Cleveland.

Rock drummer Michael Cartellone "mashed the skins" for two Damn Yankees albums (with Ted Nugent and members of Styx and Night Ranger). He currently drums for legendary rockers Lynyrd Skynyrd. *(Photo by William Rieter)*

A drummer for southern rockers Lynyrd Skynyrd and classic rock supergroup Damn Yankees, Michael Cartellone was born in Cleveland. He has played with many members of rock and roll royalty, including John Fogerty of Credence Clearwater Revival, Peter Frampton, and Cher.

The critically hailed singer-songwriter Nicholas Megalis is originally from Cleveland and was tapped by Trent Reznor to open for NIN on tour.

Pop star Kate Voegele of Bay Village has charted several singles since the release of her 2007 debut, *Don't Look Away*. Her work has been featured in the television series *One Tree Hill*.

Akron native Tim "Ripper" Owens served as the replacement for legendary Judas Priest singer Rob Halford after performing in a tribute band. His experience at least partially informs the 2001 film *Rock Star*, starring Mark Wahlberg.

Akron singer-songwriter Rachel Sweet recorded the title track to the John Waters film *Hairspray* and many of the songs for his musical *Cry Baby*.

Cleveland native and bandleader Ray Anthony was a member of legendary big band maestro Glenn Miller's band in the early 40s. Anthony also appeared in the Miller film *Sun Valley Serenade*. He went on to form his own group and is responsible for the infectious songs "The Bunny Hop" and the theme to the television drama *Dragnet*. He is perhaps best known as being the man behind the song "Hokey Pokey."

Keyboardist and songwriter Mark Avsec has been a part of the popular bands Wild Cherry, Donnie Iris and the Cruisers, and has performed with the James Gang. His song "She Don't Know Me" was recorded by New Jersey rock heavyweights Bon Jovi for their debut album.

Rock guitarist Gilby Clarke was born in Cleveland and has performed with bands as diverse as classic rockers Heart, as well as metal bands Guns N' Roses and Slash's Snakepit.

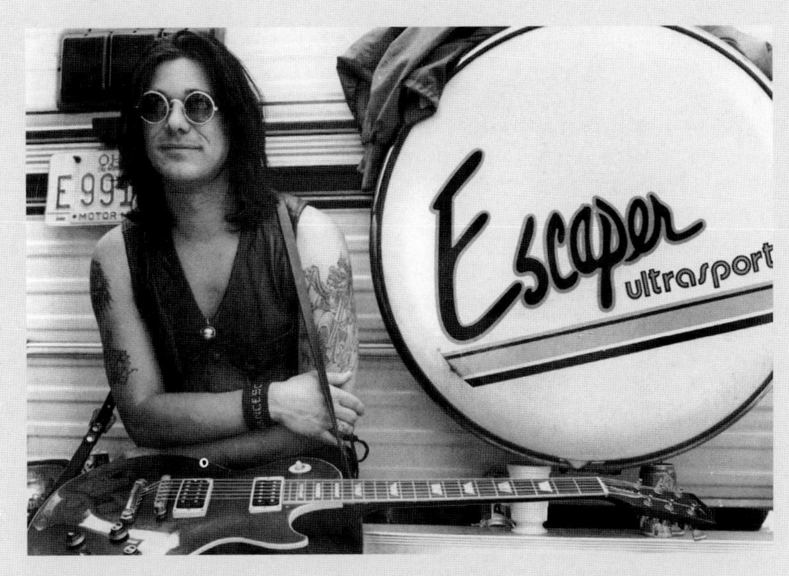

Former Guns N' Roses guitarist Gilby Clarke hangs out backstage at the Rock and Roll Hall of Fame and Museum's 1995 'Topping Off" ceremony in Cleveland. *(Photo by Janet Macoska)*

His most recent tenure in a band was in the reality television show *Rock Star Supernova* (with Tommy Lee of Motley Crue and Jason Newsted of Metallica).

The funky Motown records act The Dazz Band launched in Cleveland and scored a Top Ten Billboard hit with "Let It Whip."

Now living in Chagrin Falls, native Clevelander Sonny Geraci landed hits with the band The Outsiders ("Time Won't Let Me") and Climax ("Precious and Few").

Neil "Spyder" Giraldo is the bandleader and husband of legendary rock vocalist Pat Benatar. He was also a member of Rick Derringer's touring band. Giraldo was born in Cleveland.

Akron-born soul singer James Ingram has worked with a wide range of artists across multiple musical genres, including the legendary Ray Charles, country music icon Kenny Rogers, Quincy Jones, Natalie Cole, and Anita Baker. He co-wrote "P.Y.T. (Pretty Young Thing)" which appears on the late Michael Jackson's blockbuster album, *Thriller.*

Born Erick Lee Purkheiser in Akron, Lux Interior of the garage rock/punk act The Cramps helped create the "psychobilly" genre of rock music.

Instrumentalist Andy Kubiszewski spent the early part of his career in the Cleveland band Exotic Birds. The Cleveland Institute of Music student ended up drumming in a number of different acts, including The The, Nine Inch Nails, Crowded House, and Stabbing Westward.

Composer and Oberlin College student John Harold Kander is responsible for a series of triumphant musical theatre productions with co-writer Fred Ebb. Their work includes Broadway successes *Cabaret, Chicago,* and *Kiss of the Spider Woman.* The duo also contributed a handful of songs to the 1975 Barbra Striesand film, *Funny Lady.*

Cleveland-based singer-songwriter Kevin McMahon, recording under the moniker Prick, was a part of the seminal Cleveland band Lucky Pierre, which also featured Trent Reznor. McMahon has since toured as Prick with

Reznor and David Bowie and was once signed to Reznor's label, Nothing Records.

Cleveland-born drummer Eric Singer did a stint with Black Sabbath early in his career, replacing original drummer Bill Ward. He has performed with a laundry list of hard rock acts, including Lita Ford, Alice Cooper, and Brian May of Queen. Singer has been in the band Kiss twice, once as himself (for their *Revenge* album), and once in the Catman make-up and costuming as replacement for Peter Criss.

The diminutive Cleveland singer's reputation as a favorite of other jazz singers made him an endearing figure in that genre's scene. *(Photo by Janet Macoska)*

"Little" Jimmy Scott, the diminutive jazz singer with the unique voice, was born in Cleveland. He was known as the "jazz singer's favorite singer," earning the praise of contemporaries like Nancy Wilson, Billie Holiday, and Ray Charles.

Contemporary Christian band Relient K calls Canton home. The group has delivered a string of punk-pop music from their home base. Members of the band originally met at Malone College in Canton. Named for a Plymouth compact car model, they scored a pair of albums in the Top 20 on *Billboard* magazine's 200 album chart.

Urban contemporary vocal quartet The Rude Boys are from Cleveland and have achieved some success over the last ten years. Rude Boy Larry Marcus is a cousin of legendary blues guitar hero B.B. King.

Classical pianist and NPR radio host Christopher O'Riley calls Sagamore Hills home these days. Riley is host to the popular weekly NPR radio program *From the Top*. He achieved hit status for a pair of tribute albums to alt-rock band Radiohead.

Akron New Wave band The Waitresses are best known for their hit 1980 single "I Know What Boys Like," which didn't get discovered as a hit until 1982. The group, led by singer Patty Donahue and guitarist/chief songwriter Chris Butler, went on to record the theme for the television sitcom, *Square Pegs*.

Country singer-songwriter Tammy Cochran, best known for her single "Angels in Waiting," was born in Austinburg.

Hip-hop/rap artists Ray Cash, Ace Boogie, DJ Mick Boogie, Avant, and Kid Cudi are all from Northeast Ohio.

Oberlin College has produced a great number of musicians who have gone on to perform in popular alternative rock music acts, including The Mars Volta, Oingo Boingo, Liz Phair, Josh Ritter, The Sea and Cake, Trans Am, Tortoise, and the Yeah Yeah Yeahs.

Loud, proud, and snotty: local boy Stiv Bators raged as leader of the Cleveland punk band The Dead Boys. *(Photo by Janet Macoska)*

The influential Cleveland-based punk band The Dead Boys is best known for the histrionics of front man Stiv Bators and their single "Sonic Reducer," a song revived in the 90s by Seattle grunge band Pearl Jam.

Along with J.J. Jackson, Alan Hunter, Mark Goodman, and Martha Quinn, Rocky River High School graduate Nina Blackwood was one of the MTV Music Television network's first "vee-jays" (video jockeys).

Northeast Ohio native Rick Derringer is responsible for two of rock and roll's most enduring songs: "Hang On Sloopy" by his band The McCoys (an Ohio State University favorite) and "Rock and Roll, Hoochie Koo," which he recorded as a solo artist.

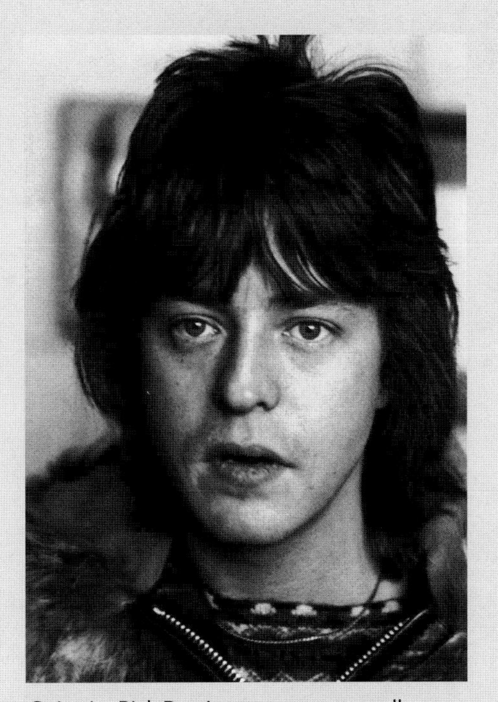

Guitarist Rick Derringer wrote two well-known songs to Ohioans — "Hang on Sloopy," played at Ohio State University football games — and "Rock and Roll, Hoochie Koo." *(Photo by Janet Macoska)*

Sports

If there's one thing Northeast Ohio natives understand, it is disappointment as it relates to professional sports. Over the course of the last four decades, we've been subjected to the psychic baggage known simply as "the Curse." There are plenty of alleged reasons for this: the Curse of Rocky Colavito; the Native American curse related to the Cleveland Indians maintaining Chief Wahoo as a mascot. However it is attributed, this "maloik" is one of the longest running in professional sports.

We definitely get our share of hearing "1964" as the last time there was a sports championship for the city. And we are regularly subjected to the once-sensational, now tired "low-light reel" of "Red Right 88," "The Drive," "The Fumble," "The Shot" and Jose Mesa blowing the 1997 World Series in the ninth inning of Game 7.

ESPN named our city the "most tortured sports city" in 2004. While it most certainly is an unfortunate moniker, it downplays and discounts the important professional sports accomplishments, athletes, coaches, and achievers that have come from the region and made a dramatic influence on professional sports.

James Nathaniel "Jim" Brown:

The legendary Cleveland Browns running back basically reinvented the position with his dominance and is widely considered the best running back in professional football history. A hulking and fast football carrier, Brown was wildly successful with the Browns; he left the NFL having broken many records, including single-season rushing yards and career rushing yards. He became the first player ever to reach 100 touchdowns (he finished with 106 rushing TDs, 126 total). Brown continues to be active in professional football (he's an Executive Advisor for the Browns) and as a social justice advocate for inner city teens trying to extract themselves from gangs and their activities. Brown also enjoyed a brief career as an actor in film and television.

Perhaps the most dominant running back in the history of the NFL, Jim Brown (left) makes a personal appearance at a Cleveland Browns event with WMJI-FM morning show host Jimmy Malone. *(Photo by Janet Macoska)*

Paul Brown:

Considered the "father of modern American football" who had "profound influence on the game" and known as the "architect of the NFL" (see Andrew O'Toole's book *The Rise and Fall and Rise Again of Football's Most Innovative Coach*), Brown came to prominence as the coach of the Cleveland Browns. Brown modernized and reinvented the game. Much of what is celebrated today in football (the sideline pass, the two-minute offense, scouting opponents, watching game film, play calling from the sidelines) took place because of Brown's implementation. He even institutionalized the college draft system. After leaving Cleveland, Brown established the Cincinnati Bengals as part of an NFL expansion. In his 17 years as coach in Cleveland, he led the team to seven championships, including five in a row, and amassed an all-time record of 158-48, a brawny .767 winning percentage.

According to some, he was the "father" of modern American football. NFL coach Paul Brown, the namesake of the Cleveland Browns, became a Northeast Ohio and American legend. *(Cleveland* Press *Collection of the Cleveland State University Libraries)*

John Heisman:

The Cleveland-born football player and coach spent a significant portion of his career at Oberlin College in the late 19th century. He did stints at the University of Akron and Buchtel College in between his tenures there. An advocate of the forward pass, Heisman was the original modernizer of the game of football; he set the table for Paul Brown to reinvent football. Heisman introduced innovations including direct snaps to the quarterback from the center, and audible signals at the line of scrimmage. Heisman was the director of New York's Downtown Athletic Club; in 1935, the club crowned him the "Best College Football Player." A year later, when Heisman passed away, the trophy was renamed after him. Today, Heisman's name is synonymous with excellence and the award is still bestowed on the best collegiate football player.

Lou Holtz:

The College Football Hall of Famer and Kent State University student is best known for being the motivational coach of the Notre Dame college football program. He led Notre Dame to the 1988 National Championship. A noted author and commentator, Holtz is the only coach in the history of NCAA football to lead six different college teams to bowl games. He's currently an analyst for ESPN.

Author/columnist David Giffels thinks that basketball superstar LeBron James some day may be as dominant on the Silver Screen as he is on the hardwood court. *(Photo by Walter Novak)*

LeBron James:

What can be said about the St. Vincent-St. Mary high school basketball phenom-turned NBA sensation for the Cleveland Cavaliers? One thing is certain: the Akron native's story is known the world over and his style of play has quickly earned him kudos and the suggestion that he could become the best player ever. An Olympic gold medal winner with the U.S. Men's Basketball team in 2008, he is the subject of a new feature film *More Than a Game* and is considered a global athletic icon.

Don King:

The Cleveland-born boxing promoter briefly attended Kent State University before pursuing his chosen career. One of his earliest promotions involved bringing world-renowned boxing legend Muhammad Ali to Cleveland for a charity bout to benefit a local hospital. King brought the sport of boxing to a whole new level of commercial prominence, including the Ali vs. George Foreman fight "The Rumble in the Jungle" and the 1975 classic "Thrilla in Manila," which pitted Ali against arch-nemesis Joe Frazier. King has promoted many of boxing's biggest names during his career, including champions Evander Holyfield, Larry Holmes, Lennox Lewis, and the troubled boxing great, "Iron" Mike Tyson.

Bobby Knight:

The feisty college basketball coach and analyst is best known as the coach of the Indiana Hoosiers, a program with which he won 11 Big Ten Conference Championships, three NCAA championships, and one National Invitation Tournament (NIT) championship. Clearly, his controversial and explosive coaching style (exemplified by the infamous chair-throwing incident for which he was charged with assault) was nonetheless a winning one. Knight was born in Massillon and started his coaching career at Cuyahoga Falls High School. He won a 1984 U.S. Olympic gold medal coaching the men's basketball team. Knight was elected to the Basketball Hall of Fame in 1991.

Bernie Kosar:

No sports figure is considered a local hero quite like the former quarterback of the Cleveland Browns. Born in Boardman,

Former Cleveland Browns quarterback Bernie Kosar trades in the football for a baseball glove at then-Jacobs Field during the 1997 Major League Baseball All-Star Game festivities. ***(Photo by Janet Macoska)***

near Youngstown, Kosar became a star quarterback at the University of Miami and publicly stated his desire to play for the Cleveland Browns, endearing him to throngs of Browns fans. In his first five years, he helped lead the team into the playoffs four times and guided them to three AFC

"I remember the run the Cleveland Indians had in the 90s when Jacobs Field was a magnet for people and downtown was just swarming with people. It was like the city just sort of exploded . . . I've always felt like Cleveland has a genuine capacity for excitement. There's such a hunger for people to experience success and victory, or even just something cool . . . It's only a question of giving the people what they want."

— *Andy Borowitz, humorist and satirist,*
The Borowitz Report

championship games. He is perhaps more beloved to the region's sports fans than the 1980 "Kardiac Kids" Browns team.

Chuck Noll:

Clevelanders are not crazy about talking about the Pittsburgh Steelers football team. But if it wasn't for Cleveland-born Steelers football coach Chuck Noll, one wonders if the Steelers' dynasty would have existed. A former player with the Cleveland Browns, Noll has more Super Bowl wins (four) than any other head coach in the history of the National Football League. He was the architect of the legendary "Steel Curtain" defense. Noll was elected to the Pro Football Hall of Fame in 1995 and is one of the most successful native Clevelanders in professional sports.

Shaquille O'Neal:

The four-time NBA champion, towering center, and media star was acquired in 2009 by the Cleveland Cavaliers in a move to help earn a National Basketball Association (NBA) championship title for the city with Akron's favorite son, LeBron James. O'Neal makes the Cavaliers the only NBA team in 2009 with multiple MVP and scoring title winners. The only thing O'Neal has more of than titles is nicknames, including "Shaq Diesel," "Kazaam," (named for one of his starring roles in a Hollywood film) and "The Big Cactus."

Jesse Owens:

He is the runner who famously embarrassed Adolph Hitler by winning four Gold Medals in the 1936 Olympics in Berlin, Germany. The Cleveland-bred Owens began breaking track records as a teenager; his records set in the Olympics were held for decades. An Ohio State University student, he went on to be the Director of Physical Education for Negroes under the office of Civilian Defense before going to work for the Ford Motor Company.

Jesse Owens dominated the 1936 Berlin Olympics, earning four gold medals for track and field events. *(Cleveland Press Collection of the Cleveland State University Libraries)*

Kelly "The Ghost" Pavlik:

Dubbed by fans and boxing pundits "The Ghost" and "The Pride of Youngstown," the boxing sensation has earned the World Boxing Council (WBC) and World Boxing Organization (WBO) middleweight championships in his short but auspicious career. He has shunned the glitz and glamour found in professional sports and maintained allegiance to his hometown. After turning pro in 2000, Pavlik won his first 26 middleweight bouts. Although recently defeated by 42-year-old middleweight Bernard "The Executioner" Hopkins, Pavlik has handily dispatched all but five of his opponents.

Pro Football Hall of Fame, Monday Night Football and the National Football League:

The National Football League (NFL) was established in Canton in 1920 as the American Professional Football Association, and the modern game began to take shape in Northeast Ohio shortly thereafter. For this reason, the Pro Football Hall of Fame officially opened in fall 1963 in Canton. Players from the NFL are inducted into the Hall every year, part of festivities that include a pre-season football game at Canton's Fawcett Stadium in August. The now-ubiquitous television coverage of the NFL called *Monday Night Football* first took place in Cleveland in a game between the Cleveland Browns and New York Jets in 1970.

Robert "Bobby" Woodward Rahal:

The Medina-born, open-wheel auto racing driver helped popularize the sport of racing in the 80s as a three-time racing champion and winner of some two dozen races in Championship Auto Racing Teams (CART). Rahal's first victory was a particularly sweet one: he won the inaugural Budweiser Cleveland 500 (which eventually became known as the Grand Prix of Cleveland). Rahal won the 1986 Indianapolis 500 as a driver and won the legendary race again as a race car owner in 2004.

Frank Robinson:

One of the all-time home run leaders in Major League Baseball (MLB), Robinson played for several different professional teams during his career, including the two World Series-winning Baltimore Orioles teams, the Cincinnati Reds, and the Cleveland Indians. Robinson has the rare distinction with the latter team: he became the first African-American major league manager (as player-manager) with the Tribe. A Baseball Hall of Fame inductee, Robinson has won two MVP awards, one World Series MVP award and was bestowed with the Presidential Medal of Freedom by President George W. Bush in 2005.

Don Shula:

Born in Grand River, Shula graduated from both John Carroll University and

"I've always been a bit suspicious of the people on the winning team. I think that's why, at least for me, there's this weird disconnect in seeing LeBron James and the Cleveland Cavaliers look so superhuman – because we don't experience that much. In L.A. and [New York], the response to sports teams is so different; they're so used to winners and being the center of attention with Hollywood and Broadway, that the expectation is always that they'll always be 'number one.' And when they're not, the fans desert them en masse. If you're not winning the Super Bowls and World Series, nobody [cares] about you, whereas in Cleveland we've been frustrated by sports for so long, it affects us differently. John Adams, who bangs a drum in the outfield at Cleveland Indians games, is the perfect emblem of Cleveland — the metaphor of a man willing to keep beating the drums, regardless of how the team is doing, says a lot about the hard-bitten devotion that Clevelanders have."

— Andy Borowitz, humorist and satirist,
The Borowitz Report

Case Western Reserve University. He is the only professional football coach to lead an NFL team to a perfect season – undefeated in the regular season schedule, through the playoffs and the Super Bowl – with the Miami Dolphins. The former Clevelander won two Super Bowls with the Dolphins after a brief stint with the Cleveland Browns as a player in the early 50s. *Sports Illustrated*'s "Sportsman of the Year" in 1993, Shula was inducted into the Pro Football Hall of Fame in 1997, capping off a career filled with dozens of distinctions.

Cleveland native and John Carroll grad Don Shula coached the only undefeated team in NFL history (Miami Dolphins), but he also played for the Cleveland Browns. *(Cleveland* Press *Collection of the Cleveland State University Libraries)*

George Steinbrenner:

Although Clevelanders might not be keen on trumpeting the successes of a New York Yankee, Steinbrenner must be mentioned. Aside from leading the most famous baseball team to championship prominence as an owner/entrepreneur, Steinbrenner was the first true commercial baseball marketer who established the New York Yankees baseball club as a global brand on par with Coca-Cola, McDonald's, and Budweiser. Born in Rocky River and briefly involved in Cleveland baseball, basketball, and politics, the man nicknamed "The Boss" is also partly responsible for inflating player salaries and causing some degree of disparity between smaller and larger market teams. Steinbrenner's entry into professional sports ownership was with the Cleveland Pipers basketball club, a team coached by the first African-American pro basketball coach, John McClendon.

New York Yankees catalyst George Steinbrenner (left) is a Cleveland native who was very active in politics before moving to New York and into professional sports ownership. *(Cleveland* Press *Collection of the Cleveland State University Libraries)*

Jim Tressel:

The Mentor-born college football coach and former Baldwin-Wallace quarterback reached coaching success with a stint at Youngstown State that led to national championships and coach of the year honors for him. Tressel made the move to head coach at Ohio State University in 2001, replacing beleaguered coach John Cooper. He has earned similar honors there with the Buckeye football program. Referred to by some as "The Vest" (for his choice of garb on game days) Tressel has won five Big Ten Championships and directed the Buckeyes to the 2002 National Championship. Tressel is the only coach to win national titles at two different schools and at two different divisional levels of NCAA football.

Paul Warfield:

The NFL wide receiver, born in Warren, holds the distinction of being the only player to play on the 1964 Cleveland Browns championship team and on the 1972 undefeated "perfect season" Miami Dolphins.

Moses Fleetwood Walker:

He was the first African-American major league baseball player. He went to Oberlin College. He played until 1889, after which Jim Crow laws prohibited African Americans from playing major league baseball professionally again until Jackie Robinson "broke" the color barrier in 1947.

Denton True "Cy" Young:

One of the most dominant baseball pitchers in the history of the major leagues, Young played nearly a century ago and still holds several of baseball's longstanding records: most career wins (511), most innings pitched (7,355), most complete games (749) and most career starts (815). An inductee into the National Baseball Hall of Fame, Young pitched for the Cleveland Spiders and Cleveland Naps and pitched the first perfect game of modern baseball. In honor of his accomplishments, the Cy Young Award was established in 1956; it is awarded to the season's best pitchers in both the American and National leagues.

"I guess if I had to say one thing [to Northeast Ohio sports fans] it would be, 'Lighten up. Enjoy the games, win or lose, have a good time, and just keep in mind you don't know as much as you think you know about professional sports.'"

— Joe Tait, legendary Cleveland Cavaliers broadcaster

Did You Know?

Born in Akron, Ara Parseghian is the winningest coach in the history of Notre Dame football.

English Premier League goaltender for Aston Villa and former U.S. soccer team goalie Brad Friedel is perhaps Bay Village's most famous athlete.

Ron Jaworski was born in Youngstown. The ESPN NFL analyst was the former quarterback of the Philadehphia Eagles.

LeBron James is the first NBA MVP in league history to lead his team in points, rebounds, assists, blocks, and steals in the same season.

Legendary pitcher and 1937 Baseball Hall of Fame inductee Cy Young won 317 games after the age of 30.

As sports go, mixed martial arts is relatively new in popularity, but the Cleveland-born Mac Danzig is already an Ultimate Fighting Championship titleholder.

Glenville High School grad and Cleveland native Troy Smith is an NFL quarterback, most recently with the Baltimore Ravens. He played at Ohio State University under coach Jim Tressel and won the 2006 Heisman Trophy and the 2006 Associated Press Player of the Year Award.

Golfer, Stow native, and Kent State University graduate Ben Curtis achieved his most famous victory in the 2003 British Open golf tournament.

Akron's favorite son LeBron James won the 2008-2009 NBA Most Valuable Player Award. Already a force in the NBA, he is poised to be one of the league's single most dominant players ever. *(Photo by Janet Macoska)*

Cleveland Indians player Tris Speaker was one of the first professional baseball players inducted into the Baseball Hall of Fame. Speaker was voted in during the second induction year.

Cleveland Indians pitcher and Northeast Ohio resident Bob Feller was inducted into the Baseball Hall of Fame in 1962 in his first year of eligibility with an impressive 266 wins despite having lost three years of playing time due to his service in World War II.

One-time Cleveland Naps and Cleveland Indians baseball player "Shoeless" Joe Jackson is best known for his involvement in the 1919 Chicago White Sox "Black Sox" scandal of fixing the World Series. Although he earned impressive stats in his career – he has the third highest batting average in professional baseball history – Jackson is still ineligible for induction to the Baseball Hall of Fame.

Youngstown native Ray "Boom-Boom" Mancini was the lightweight boxing champion for two years during the 80s. He earned his nickname from his father, Lenny "Boom Boom" Mancini, who was also a professional boxer. The younger Mancini's wild fighting style became popular and was adopted by several other boxers of the time.

Current Cleveland resident and famed Olympic "Magnificent Seven" gymnast Dominique Moceanu won a gold medal as a part of the 1996 U.S. Olympic Gymnastics team.

Former Cleveland Indians player and manager Mike Hargrove is best known as "Grover" to more recent fans with World Series memories. But he had another nickname first: "The Human Rain Delay." Named for his fidgety routine before nearly every pitch he faced as a player, Hargrove would adjust his batting glove, jersey, pants, and batter's helmet before carefully planting each foot in the batter's box. This routine preempted every pitch, giving opposing pitchers, managers, and umpires fits.

Ozzie Newsome's pain over the failed Red Right 88 play in the end zone was shared by sports fans across the region. That play, along with the heartbreakers that came after it, "The Drive," "The Fumble," and "The Shot," have become an integral part of the Greater Cleveland lexicon. *(Cleveland* Press *Collection of the Cleveland State University Libraries)*

On the "Local" Tip & Northeast Ohio Lingo

Some of Northeast Ohio's most interesting popular culture events and pioneers either didn't make a huge splash outside of the region, or made the kind of splash many are not too terribly fond of remembering.

"Big Chuck" Schodowski, Bob "Hoolihan the Weatherman" Wells, and "L'il Jon" Rinaldi:

These three pioneering, late-night television hosts never broke free from Northeast Ohio to a broader national audience, but their jokes, skits, and laugh tracks continue to humor fans of the show and their diehard consciousness. Schodowski worked for a long time with Ernie "Gholuardi" Anderson. Schodowski and Wells became Ghoulardi's replacement after Anderson's character was retired and he moved to California. Working as a duo (with Rinaldi replacing Wells in 1979) "Big Chuck & L'il John" did a variety of parodies and ethnic humor skits, some of which are still popular, including "Ben Crazy" and the "Kielbasa Kid." These over-the-top humor shorts helped move along a slate of B-grade horror, suspense, and action flicks for many years.

Local late-night TV luminaries "Big Chuck and L'il John" pose for the paparazzi with one of Cleveland's favorite sons, Drew Carey. *(Photo by Janet Macoska)*

"Barnaby" (a.k.a. Linn Sheldon):

His "Hi neighbor" was a greeting as familiar to kids in Northeast Ohio as that of his nationwide counterpart, Fred "Mister" Rogers. Sheldon's morning program for kids (complete with invisible pet parrot) graced WUAB-TV in Cleveland for a long time. If you're over 40, odds are you watched him more than once during your youth.

Roldo Bartimole:

His motto is "Tell the truth and shame the devils," as is quoted on the Cleveland Memory website. The Cleveland native's journalism over the last five decades has become synonymous with exposing inequity, corruption, and back-room dealings in Northeast Ohio, particularly as it relates to Cuyahoga's county seat. No less an authority than consumer protection activist/advocate and perennial presidential candidate Ralph Nader has proclaimed an appreciation for Bartimole's oversight on matters of governmental, corporate, and ruling class assults on the region's citizenry. Bartimole's work has appeared in the city's many alternative newsweekly papers and in his own newsletter, *Point of View*. An inductee of the Cleveland Press Club Hall of Fame, Bartimole is beloved by his readers. *Cleveland Magazine* called him "the poor man's [American revolutionary] Tom Paine."

City of Cleveland Default, Ralph Perk and Dennis Kucinich:

In 1978, Cleveland was the first major U.S. city to default on its debts since the Great Depression, when $15 million in loans from local banks came due. It was the direct result of a down economy, a flight in population from the city that had started in the late 50s, and Ralph Perk, the prior mayor, having run up almost $30 million dollars worth of debt. The default happened on the next mayor's – Dennis Kucinich's – watch. His attempt to settle the debts with the local banks was to no avail and the city remained in default until 1987. Perk is best known for having set his own hair on fire with a welder's torch at a ribbon-cutting ceremony; Kucinich became a member of the U.S. House of Representatives and ran for president in 2004 and 2008. And Cleveland?

Well, let's agree that some of its troubles dating back to 1978 (like urban flight, lost manufacturing and other jobs, and population loss) still exist today.

Cleveland Municipal Stadium and the "World Series of Rock":

Though it may be long gone (demolished after Art Modell moved the Cleveland Browns to Baltimore) Cleveland Municipal Stadium hosted world-class professional sports. Anyone born prior to the 90s in Northeast Ohio likely has a memory of the venerable outdoor venue through Indians and/or Browns games. Cleveland Stadium also hosted a prestigious slate of rock concert spectacles by The Beatles, The Rolling Stones, The Who, Pink Floyd, Paul McCartney, and a day-long concert launch of the Rock and Roll Hall of Fame and Museum that featured dozens of famous entertainers. The stadium also featured the "World Series of Rock," a Belkin Productions concert event that ran intermittently from 1974 to 1980 and showcased big-name acts like Crosby, Stills, Nash & Young, Emerson, Lake &

Frampton Comes Alive: guitarist Peter Frampton (top reft) rocks out at Cleveland Municipal Stadium for one of the many installments of the "World Series of Rock" concerts created by local concert promoters Belkin Productions. *(Photo by Janet Macoska)*

Palmer, Rod Stewart, Aerosmith, Ted Nugent, Fleetwood Mac, AC/DC, Journey, Def Leppard, and Peter Frampton, among others.

"Cleveland Weather":

By now we all know that the summers in Northeast Ohio are short ones and, as much as we all love him, veteran meteorologist Dick Goddard really can't control the weather. The white-outs/blizzards at Cleveland Indians home openers and "seven month winters," to quote *Plain Dealer* Minister of Culture Michael Heaton, definitely leave their mark and have a say in how we all view (and live in) the region. Some people call it "Cleveland Weather," but really, winter hammers everyone here. By February, even the most hearty souls are ready for some sunshine.

Cuyahoga River Fire "The Burning River":

Since the Cuyahoga River went up in flames due to an oil slick in June 1969, comedians have used the event as the most prevalent touchstone to get their digs in on Cleveland. But were it not for that event, the environmental movement might not be what it is today. The fire itself was a largely underwhelming event, but underscored the premise that protecting natural resources should be a priority for the U.S. The fire set in motion a string of environmentally conscious events and decisions that included the establishment of an annual Earth Day, the U.S. Environmental Protection Agency, and the Clean Water Act.

Gary Dee

The controversial radio show host born Gary David Gilbert was a pioneering figure in talk radio and a forerunner to the "shock jock" phenomenon. With stints at the microphone at Cleveland stations WERE-AM, WHK-AM, and WWWE (a.k.a. "3WE," now known as WTAM-AM), Dee delved headfirst into politics, religion, and the news of the day in a satirical manner and implemented country music and a good ol' boy approach to his listeners. While Dee did make attempts to broaden his horizons in the larger Washington, D.C. and New York City markets, he never quite gained the traction he had in Cleveland with his approach. He died in November 1995 after a brief return to Cleveland radio.

Dick Feagler:

One of Cleveland's most well-respected news reporters, anchors, and commentators, Feagler is the recipient of dozens of journalism awards and has penned columns and news stories over a multi-decade career. Some of his better columns during his tenures at The *Plain Dealer* and now-defunct The Cleveland *Press* have been collected in book form in *Feagler's Cleveland*. A winner of 23 Emmy awards and a 1991 Peabody Award, Feagler's commentaries have appeared on Cleveland's WKYC-TV 3 and WEWS-TV 5, and on his half-hour public television program *Feagler & Friends*.

Dorothy Fuldheim:

Perhaps Cleveland's most well-respected news reporter, commentator, anchor, and feminist, Fuldheim was actually the first U.S. female news reporter and commentator as well. A native of Cleveland Heights, Fuldheim won countless journalism awards for her work and interviewed scores of

Legendary Cleveland journalist Dorothy Fuldheim interviews Bob Hope during a televised segment on WEWS-TV. The marquee value of many of Fuldheim's interview subjects was staggering. *(Cleveland* Press *Collection of the Cleveland State University Libraries)*

important newsmakers before retiring. Among her most famous interviews: German dictator Adolph Hitler, Italian dictator Benito Mussolini, Martin Luther King, Jr., and Helen Keller.

"Ghoulardi" (a.k.a. Ernie Anderson):

For a period of three years, Anderson hosted Shock Theater, a late-night television show that featured a B-grade horror movie of the week, bookended by radically weird skits. His alter ego "Ghoulardi," who hosted the show, was like a crazy, comic-book blend of Screamin' Jay Hawkins, beatnik poets, jazz hepcats, and a kitschy version of what the devil might look like if hell was a crushed red velvet lounge. The blend of humor and macabre made "Ghoulardi" and Anderson legendary in Cleveland and among Northeast Ohio natives.

"Stay sick!" Ernie Anderson's "Ghoulardi" character is still so popular after all these years that the former Clevelander is celebrated here with an annual Ghoulardifest. *(Cleveland* Press *Collection of the Cleveland State University Libraries)*

Dick Goddard:

The "marathon man" of Cleveland television, Goddard has been the city's most trusted weatherman (and animal adoption advocate/pet lover) for over four decades. Born in Akron, Goddard is a jack of all trades, along with being a meteorologist. He's authored a couple of books and is recognized for his work as an illustrator and Cleveland Browns statistician. He also helms the annual Woolybear Festival in Vermilion (it started in Birmingham in the early 70s) which celebrates a black-and-orange striped caterpillar. It continues to draw over 100,000 people annually. He is the longest active member of the American Meteorological Society, and he occasionally turns up on Tony Rizzo's *Rizzo on the Radio* show as a special guest.

The Hough Riots:

In summer 1966, racial tensions escalated in the Hough neighborhood of Cleveland and resulted in hundreds of fires, arrests, and dozens of injuries. In the midst of the melee, four African Americans were mortally wounded. It was seen by many as a catalyst of, or at least a leading reason for, urban sprawl and "white flight."

Kent State Shootings:

Often referred to as the "May Fourth Massacre," the Kent State University student protest of the U.S. invasion of Cambodia turned ugly when the Ohio National Guard shot some of the demonstrators, killing four and injuring nine others. A huge public outcry came forth against U.S. President Richard Nixon and Ohio Governor James A. Rhodes, the latter of whom called in the Guard to help maintain peace. Protests at college campuses across the country followed. After the shootings, Kent State's Center for Applied Conflict Management (CACM) emerged as one of the first conflict management/resolution programs for undergraduates in the U.S.

John Lanigan and the WUAB-TV *Prize Movie*:

Perhaps Cleveland's most recognized radio celebrity, Lanigan is currently part of the "Lanigan & Malone" program on WMJI-FM. He has spent more than three decades on the air here delivering a mix of current events, opinions, and (during his heyday) controversial style. He also hosted the WUAB-TV *Prize Movie* program in Cleveland, offering viewers opportunities to cash in on their trivia knowledge during breaks in the films he hosted.

Michael Stanley Band:

The biggest rock band to never emerge from the Midwest, the Michael Stanley Band is a beloved Northeast Ohio classic. The band was founded in the mid-70s and is best known for the songs "My Town," "He Can't Love You," and "In The Heartland," and for setting the attendance records at Blossom Music Center in Cuyahoga Falls and at the now-defunct Richfield Coliseum. Stanley, a Cleveland-born, Rocky River-bred and Hiram College-educated rocker, was quite successful regionally. The band broke up in 1986. Today, various incarnations join Stanley onstage for his local headlining performances with his band, The Resonators. Stanley is currently a disc jockey at WNCX 98.5 FM in Cleveland and has hosted a handful of local TV programs.

"Mistake by the Lake":

The all-encompassing comedic slam and butt-end of national jokes, this term summarizes the rust-belt decline in Cleveland over the last four decades: pollution, financial instability, race riots, manufacturing decline, and population loss.

The Morning Exchange:

The archetype and blueprint for daily morning television programming, this long-running morning show, hosted by Fred Griffith and a shifting cast of other personalities on Cleveland's WEWS-TV Channel 5, was local programming at its best. The show attracted huge audiences during its heyday. *Exchange* was used as a template for attracting a larger national audience with ABC's *Good Morning America*.

Eliot Ness:

The celebrated Cleveland lawman and Public Safety Director during the Prohibition era was a Cleveland Heights resident. Known as "the cop who couldn't be broken," Ness achieved his greatest fame in Chicago when he brought down Al Capone. Ness's career was later immortalized in the television series *The Untouchables* and in a motion picture of the same name starring Kevin Costner and Sean Connery. After his time in the Windy City, he came to Cleveland as the city's Public Safety Director. He then unsuccessfully ran for mayor of Cleveland in the mid-40s.

The "Untouchable" Eliot Ness was a famed Cleveland pop culture figure who was later portrayed in film by Kevin Costner. *(Cleveland* Press *Collection of the Cleveland State University Libraries)*

Terry Pluto:

This award-winning sports journalist and two-time Pulitzer Prize nominee went to high school at Benedictine and graduated from Cleveland State University. Once a scribe for the Akron *Beacon Journal*, he recently joined Cleveland's daily, The *Plain Dealer*. The author of over 20 critically acclaimed books, Pluto is most certainly prolific. When Pluto observes something happening in Cleveland sports, people take notice.

Jane Scott:

The first established rock music writer/critic got her start at The *Plain Dealer* in the early 60s, covering a teen music sensation called The Beatles. It is hard to say whether the notion of popular music critique or the subsequent surge of female entertainment journalists thereafter was entirely her doing, but this author would like to think that the groundbreaking "teen music columnist" paved the way for everyone from Lester Bangs to the reporters on *Entertainment Tonight*. A local legend by any measure, and a well-known and well-respected ally to musicians all over the world, Scott is a Lakewood native.

Rock and Roll Hall of Famer Bobby Womack and legendary Cleveland rock journalist Jane Scott share a moment at the Rock Hall's "Topping Off" ceremony in 1995. *(Photo by Janet Macoska)*

Subject of the most controversial murder case Northeast Ohio has ever seen, Dr. Sam Sheppard never fully recovered from the experience — even after he was exonerated. *(Cleveland* Press *Collection of the Cleveland State University Libraries)*

Local B-movie host Marty Sullivan was a Cleveland staple on weekend afternoons as "Superhost." *(Peter Chakerian collection)*

Dr. Sam Sheppard:

The Bay Village (via Cleveland Heights) native was convicted of murdering his wife Marilyn in 1954; the ongoing legal drama surrounding Sheppard drew national attention and inspired several books about the case and supposedly resulted in the television show and movie *The Fugitive* (that myth that has since been debunked). After ten years in prison, Sheppard was re-tried and found not guilty, but the ruination of his life had been realized long before his conviction was overturned. Irony of ironies, Sheppard went on to become a professional wrestler known as "The Killer."

"Superhost" (a.k.a. Marty Sullivan):

Once a local news reporter, the affable Sullivan parodied the Siegel and Shuster creation Superman to some degree in his comedic, Saturday afternoon movie show. A recipient of a Silver Circle Award from the National Academy of Television Arts and Sciences, "Superhost" helmed a four-hour show on Saturday afternoons starting at noon on Cleveland's WUAB-TV. He usually screened two films, in conjunction with Leon Errol and *Three Stooges* shorts. He was also known for his own host of comic parodies.

"Super Radio" WIXY-AM 1260

The station lasted for just over a decade, yet it had a major impact on the Cleveland radio market. WIXY holds a special place in Northeast Ohio music lore, partly because it featured great air personalities like Larry Morrow, "Big" Jack Armstrong, and Billy Bass and sponsored legendary concerts (including bringing The Beatles to Cleveland for two famous concerts).

Joe Tait and "Ten Cent Beer Night":

The legendary "Voice of the Cleveland Cavaliers" has been a broadcasting institution in Northeast Ohio for more than four decades. He even called Cleveland Indians baseball games for a short time as well. His most famous calls to date are probably the Cleveland Cavaliers' 2007 NBA Eastern Conference title game against the Detroit Pistons and the bedlam that ensued during a beer promotion at the June 1974 game between the Indians and Texas Rangers. Tait's five-word calling card "Wham! with the right hand" is synonymous with Cavaliers basketball and a key part of the Northeast Ohio vernacular. Tait lives in Medina County.

Ever since Cleveland gained its NBA basketball franchise in 1970, Joe Tait has been the most enduring presence in the Cavalier universe. It is hard for a Cleveland basketball fan to think of Cavs games without also thinking about the great job Tait has done behind the radio microphone. *(Photo courtesy of the Cleveland Cavaliers)*

"The Really Big Show" with Tony Rizzo:

Also known as "Rizzo on the Radio," this two-hour morning sports and pop culture show on ESPN 850 WKNR-AM carries forth many of the traditions that Rizzo, a longtime Cleveland sports broadcasting staple, used from his WHK-AM and WMJI-FM days. The show features regular callers, sound bites, inside jokes (like despondent Cleveland sports fans joking about jumping from the I-480 highway bridge), and segments like "Trivia Tuesday," "Free Food Friday," "Survey Wednesday," and "Who Said That?" It is as much about nothing (in that *Seinfeld* sort of way) as it is about Cleveland professional sports. Rizzo and producer Josh Sabo even have Assistant Program Director Aaron Goldhammer (a Denver native, Broncos fan, and Ohio State Buckeye hater) as a foil and arch nemesis. The program has the legs to become legendary.

The Full Cleveland:

It is something of a slang term and sartorial slam, but it is sometimes applied as a definition to the city itself. In fashion terminology, the "Full Cleveland" was a tacky, 70s-era dress suit that included a white patent leather, vinyl, or plastic belt, and matching white shoes. No one is really sure where the term actually started, but then again, no one really dresses like this, either. At least not out in public.

Mike Trivisonno:

Once a wiseacre caller nicknamed "Mr. Know-It-All" on WWWE-AM sportscaster Pete Franklin's show, Trivisonno has transcended his telephone antics with a lengthy career in Cleveland radio as a host. "Triv," as he's known to his listeners, rants on everything from sports to politics and all points in between. Trivisonno broadcasts on WTAM-AM 1100 and sits as the latest in a line of talk radio pundits (see Cleveland radio staples Franklin and WHK ranter-and-raver Gary Dee) who apparently relishes pushing his listeners' buttons.

Like a futuristic record player, the Rock and Roll Hall of Fame and Museum cuts into the Cleveland skyline from this Lake Erie view. *(Photo by Janet Macoska)*

Did You Know? **The "Concert for the Hall of Fame" celebrating the opening of the Rock and Roll Hall of Fame and Museum in 1995 featured some of the final performances by legends Johnny Cash and The Kinks.**

Credits

This book would not have been possible without the help, support, and guidance of Deanna Adams, Chris Andrikanich, Steven "Thank you, sir" Batten, Charles Burkett, Tad Carper, George Carr, Bruce Chamberlin, T.L. Champion, Hazel Chapman, Cleveland SPJ, Cleveland Public Library, Cleveland State University Library, Larry Collins, Karen Cook and Terry Provost, Debra Darnall, Eric and Cynthia Eakin, Tom Feran, Kelly Ferjutz, Judith Fisher Freed, Glenn Gamboa, The Gecewich Family, David Giffels, Jeff Giles, Leigh Goldie, John Gorman, David Gray and the staff at Gray and Company, Kymberli Hagelberg, John "Radio" Hannibal, Michael Heaton, Patricia Heaton, Derek Hess, Wendy Hoke, Scott Huler, Jennifer Keirn, Steven Kotler, Don Kriss, Jane Lassar, Steven Liss, Rob Lucas, Scott Malchus, Calondra McArthur, David Lee Morgan, Jr., Mike Olszewski, Marc Tyler Nobleman, Michael Norman, Kay Moran Panovec, Jason Pettigrew, Karen Robinson, Dave Schwensen, Joseph Sheppa, Jim Szatkowski, Claudia J. Taller, Joe Tait, Paul Tepley, Elmer Turner, Kathy Vogel, Matt Wardlaw, Tom Wilson, Chuck Yarborough, and Jarrod Zickefoose.

Very special thanks to Layne Anderson, Mark "Munch" Bishop, Kelsey Brubaker, Michael and Monica and Will Chakerian, Pete and Ruth Chakerian, Brittyn DeWerth, Josh Donald and Callie Scott, the Giffords, Lance and Mary Beth Healy, Luke and Kate Healy, Joy and Chris Klein, Janet Macoska, Thomas Mulready and Carol Hunt, George Nemeth and McKala Everett, Vern Morrison, Walter Novak, Bill Reiter, the Sandbridge Breakfast Club, Sandy VandeVelde, and Carlo Wolff and Karen Sandstrom. Extra special thanks to the Department of Popular Culture at Bowling Green State University and The Institute on Popular Culture for Education at Syracuse University. And lastly, props to "Comma" for keeping me motivated — all without lifting a finger. Keep 'em in stitches, big man. C-Ya! Get rocked!

A very big thank you to Greg Deegan and Jim Toman of Cleveland Landmarks Press, Inc. for the opportunity.

And lastly (but definitely not least) to my wonderful family — this book would not have been possible without your love and support.

Sources

Books

Studio Cards: Funny Greeting Cards and People Who Created Them by Dean Norman (Beaver Creek Features)

Cleveland Stadium: The Last Chapter by James A. Toman and Gregory G. Deegan (Cleveland Landmarks Press)

Cleveland Rock and Roll Memories by Carlo Wolff (Gray & Company Publishers)

Moon Guide to Cleveland by Douglas Trattner (Moon Publishing)

Rock 'N' Roll and the Cleveland Connection by Deanna R. Adams (Kent State University Press)

We Are Devo! by Jade Dellinger and David Giffels (SAF Publishing, LTD.)

Big Beat Heat: Alan Freed and the Early Years of Rock & Roll by John A. Jackson (Schirmer Books)

The Buzzard by John Gorman with Tom Feran (Gray & Company Publishers)

Made in America: Eight Great All-American Creations by Murray I. Suid (Addison-Wesley)

Boys of Steel: The Creators of Superman by Marc Tyler Nobleman (Knopf Books for Young Readers)

LeBron James: Rise of a Star by David Lee Morgan, Jr. (Gray & Company Publishers)

The Franchise: LeBron James and the Remaking of the Cleveland Cavaliers by Terry Pluto and Brian Windhorst (Gray & Company Publishers)

Paul Brown: The Man Who Invented Modern Football by George Cantor (Triumph)

The Rise and Fall and Rise Again of Football's Most Innovative Coach by Andrew O'Toole (Clerisy Press)

Ghoulardi: Inside Cleveland TV's Wildest Ride by Tom Feran and R.D. Heldenfels (Gray & Company, Publishers)

Big Chuck: My Favorite Stories from 47 Years on Cleveland TV by Chuck Schodowski with Tom Feran (Gray & Company, Publishers)

The Encyclopedia of Cleveland History by David D. Van Tassel and John J. Grabowski (Indiana University Press)

The Dictionary of Cleveland Biography by David D. Van Tassel and John J. Grabowski (Indiana University Press)

Radio Daze by Mike Olszewski (Kent State University Press)

Online

All online research resources last visited July 13, 2009

2009: The Year of the River http://www.cuyahogariverrap.org/YOTR/yotr.html

PBS: Return of the Cuyahoga http://www.pbs.org/thereturnofthecuyahoga

Schumann's Cleveland Pages: http://re.cleveland.oh.us/archives/20000204.html

"Writer's Plight Sparks Outpouring" – *Plain Dealer*/Cleveland.com, March 2007
http://blog.cleveland.com/earlyedition/2007/03/writers_plight_sparks_outpouri.html

Michael Stanley Band timeline – *Plain Dealer*/Cleveland.com
http://www.cleveland.com/music/index_story.ssf?/music/more/local/timeline/sidebar/msb.html

Kaye Ballard on the Muppets: http://muppet.wikia.com/wiki/Episode_123:_Kaye_Ballard

The Id and I: http://www.theidandi.blogspot.com

"Trent Reznor in Cleveland" – *Plain Dealer*/Cleveland.com
http://www.cleveland.com/music/index_story.ssf?/music/more/local/timeline/sidebar/down.html

"Drew Carey eager for his Shakespearian debut with the Cleveland Orchestra" – *Plain Dealer*/Cleveland.com, June 2008
http://www.cleveland.com/arts/index.ssf/2008/07/drew_carey.html

Wile E. Coyote v. Roadrunner: http://www.legalnews.net/quotes/wilee.htm

Entertainment Weekly: The Pop of King - Stephen King's Top Book Picks for 2006 http://www.ew.com/ew/article/0,,1567780,00.html

"Lost Novel is Final Gift from Science Fiction Great Roger Zelazny" - SanduskyRegister.com
http://www2.sanduskyregister.com/blogs/jackson-street-beat/lost-novel-final-gift-science-fiction-great-roger-zelazny

Cleveland.com's "Homegrown Heroes" http://www.cleveland.com/homegrown/

AlanFreed.com: http://www.alanfreed.com/archives/RRHoF/936%20Ashes%20Moved%203-22-02.pdf

Hal Holbrook biography: http://pac.unlv.edu/pdf/53_halholbrookbiography.pdf

"On the Lower East Side with Jim Jarmusch" – *The New York Times*/NYTimes.com
http://www.nytimes.com/1992/04/30/garden/on-the-lower-east-side-with-jim-jarmusch-film-as-life-and-vice-versa.
html?sec=&spon=&pagewanted=all

Cleveland.About.com "Films and Filmmakers" page: http://cleveland.about.com/od/filmsandfilmmakers/tp/clevelandmovies.htm

City of Akron Fast Facts: http://www.ci.akron.oh.us/fastfacts.html

City-Data.com - Famous Ohioans: http://www.city-data.com/states/Ohio-Famous-ohioans.html

"That Was Invented in Cleveland, too?" - John Carroll University website http://www.jcu.edu/chemistry/naosmm/2007/Inventions.html

"Automobile Capital of the World? Sure, in 1902!" - John Carroll University website
http://www.jcu.edu/chemistry/naosmm/2007/AutoCapital.html

"Clarence A. Crane," Ohio History Central, July 28, 2006, http://www.ohiohistorycentral.org/entry.php?rec=2634

"Stouffer Corporation", *Ohio History Central*, July 1, 2005, http://www.ohiohistorycentral.org/entry.php?rec=991

Autospies.Com Study Auto Survey: http://www.autospies.com/news/Study-Finds-Americans-Own-2-28-Vehicles-Per-Household-26437/
Radio/TV Entry on About.com: http://radio.about.com/cs/radiodatabases/qt/blhowmanystatio.htm

Cleveland Museum of Art Kids Page: http://www.clevelandart.org/Kids/story/people/index.html

Ashtabula County Bar Association: http://www.ashtabulacountybar.com/famous_attorneys.htm

Cleveland Heights Historical Society: http://www.chhistory.org

Brad Meltzer website: http://www.bradmeltzer.com/2008/09/siegel-shuster-society.html

SupermanLand.com/Siegel & Shuster Society: http://www.supermanland.com/

North American Travel Journalists Association Conference Page: https://natja.org/conference/2009/cleveland

Positively Cleveland - About Cleveland: History http://www.positivelycleveland.com/about_cleveland/cleveland_history/

Amaraillo.com: "Why He's the Human Rain Delay" http://www.amarillo.com/stories/071208/mlb_10761492.shtml

Other Sources

Quotes from Andy Borowitz, Joe Tait, Judith Fisher Freed, Steven Kotler, David Giffels, Michael Heaton, Deanna R. Adams and Jason Pettigrew were from personally conducted interviews.

Wikipedia, Film.com, The Internet Movie Database, the All Music Guide, Encarta, and Encyclopedia Britannica Online were all consulted to confirm proper names, titles, dates, timelines and other general information related to book's encyclopedic entries.

Phil Donahue photo use approved by Creative Commons 2.0: http://www.flickr.com/photos/51035624826@N01/1363449219

Index

About the Author

Peter Chakerian is an award-winning writer, reporter and journalist. In over 18 years, his byline has appeared in The *Plain Dealer*, Akron *Beacon Journal*, *Sun Newspapers*, *Cleveland Magazine*, *Northern Ohio Live*, *Scene Magazine*, *Cleveland Free Times*, *CoolCleveland.com* and many other publications across the Midwest. He also contributes to the pop culture websites *Addicted to Vinyl*, *Blogcritics* and *Popdose*. A lifelong Northeast Ohio resident, he lives in Bay Village, Ohio, with his wife, Susan, and children Christopher and Megan.

(Photo by Layne Anderson)